Best Garden Plants *for* Tennessee

Dr. Sue Hamilton

Laura Peters

Lone Pine Publishing International

The Distributor: Lone Pine Publishing
1808 B Street NW, Suite 140
Auburn, WA, USA 98001

Website: www.lonepinepublishing.com

Library and Archives Canada Cataloguing in Publication

Hamilton, Sue L., 1958–
    Best garden plants for Tennessee / Sue L. Hamilton, Laura Peters.

Includes index.
ISBN–13: 978–976–8200–08–2
ISBN–10: 976–8200–08–1

    1. Plants, Ornamental—Tennessee. 2. Gardening—Tennessee.
I. Peters, Laura, 1968– II. Title.

SB453.2.T2H34 2006   635'.09768   C2005–906877–9

Scanning & Electronic Film: Elite Lithographers Co.

Front cover photographs by Tim Matheson and Tamara Eder except where noted. *Clockwise from top right:* Graham Thomas rose, flowering crabapple, iris, Carolina silverbell, daylily, ipomoea, daylily (*Allison Penko*), lily (*Laura Peters*), coreopsis, lily (*Erika Flatt*).

Photography: All photos by Tim Matheson, Tamara Eder and Laura Peters, except:
Doris Baucom 25a; Pam Beck 86; Sandra Bit 83a; David Cavagnaro 120a; Janet Davis 59a; Therese D'Monte 131b; Jen Fafard 126a; Derek Fell 53b, 62a, 80, 97a, 119a, 131a, 156, 166; Erika Flatt 121a, 122b, 146a, 162b; Anne Gordon 118b; Saxon Holt 53a, 67, 69a, 105a; Duncan Kelbaugh 122a; Liz Klose 167a; Debra Knapke 151a; Dawn Loewen 64a, 72b; Janet Loughrey 169a; Marilynn McAra 126b, 127b; Missouri Botanical Plantfinder 59b; Kim O'Leary 9a, 19a&b, 82a, 84a&b, 117a&b, 124a, 138b; Allison Penko 17b, 35a, 48a, 71a, 83b, 89b, 90b, 91a&b, 94a&b, 95a&b, 96b, 110b, 112b, 113a, 121b&c, 125a, 129a, 153b, 155, 157, 159b, 167b; Photos.com 127a; Reiner Richter 103; Robert Ritchie 38b, 88a, 101a, 115a, 138a; Gene Sasse-Weeks Roses 101b; Leila Sidi 132b; Mark Turner 133, 169b; Valleybrook Gardens 151b; Don Williamson 123a&b.

This book is not intended as a 'how-to' guide for eating garden plants. No plant or plant extract should be consumed unless you are certain of its identity and toxicity and of your potential for allergic reactions.

PC: P13

Table of Contents

Introduction 4

Annuals 11

Perennials 31

Trees & Shrubs 59

Roses 111

Vines 121

Bulbs 129

Herbs 141

Ferns, Grasses & Groundcovers 155

Glossary 171
Index 172
Author Biographies and Acknowledgments . . .176

Introduction

Starting a garden can seem like a daunting task. Which plants should you choose? Where should you put them in the garden? This book is intended to give beginning gardeners the information they need to start planning and planting gardens of their own. It describes a wide variety of plants and provides basic planting information such as where and how to plant.

Tennessee has a wide diversity of ecological regions, each with its unique challenges. Each region has a winter temperature range that indicates which plants will likely be hardy there. Consider this: 5° F for a plant is very different with snow cover or without, in soggy soil or in dry, and following a hot summer or a long, cold, wet one. Such factors are at least as important to plant survival as is temperature.

Hardiness zones and frost dates are two concepts often used when discussing climate. Hardiness zones are based on the average low temperatures and conditions in winter. Plants are rated based on the hardiness zones in which they can grow successfully. The average last frost date in spring combined with the average first frost date in fall allows us to predict the length of the growing season. Recognizing the type of climate where you garden helps determine which plants you can expect to survive winter. Your local garden center should be able to provide you with local cold hardiness zones and frost date information.

Getting Started

When planning your garden, start with a quick analysis of the garden as it is now. Plants have varied requirements, and it is easier to put the right plant in the right place than to change your garden to suit the plants you want.

Knowing which parts of your garden receive the most and least amounts of sunlight helps you choose the appropriate plants for these locations. The amount of sun a site receives is generally described with the following terms: full sun (direct, unobstructed light for all or most of the day); partial shade (direct sun for about half the day and shade for the rest); light shade (shade for all or most of the day, with some sun filtering through to ground level); and full shade (no direct sunlight). It's important that you match a plant's light requirement to its intended location, but many can adapt to a range of light levels.

Plants use soil to hold themselves upright, but they also rely on the many resources it holds: air, water, nutrients, organic matter and a host of microbes. The particle size of the soil influences the amount of air, water and nutrients it can hold. Sand, with the largest particles, has a lot of air space and allows water and nutrients to drain quickly. Clay, with the smallest particles, is high in nutrients but has very little air space. Water is therefore slow to penetrate clay and slow to drain from it. In general, Tennessee tends to have clay soils, and only a limited palette of plants tolerate clay soil. As a result, gardeners would do well to improve their soil with compost before planting.

Compost is one of the best and most important amendments you can add to any type of soil. Compost improves soil by adding organic matter and nutrients, introducing soil microbes, increasing water retention and improving drainage. Compost can be purchased, or you can make it in your own backyard.

Soil acidity or alkalinity (measured on the pH scale) influences the nutrients available to plants. A pH of 7 is neutral; a lower pH is more acidic. Most plants prefer a soil with a pH of 5.5–7.5. Soil-testing kits to determine your soil's pH, nutrient content and percentage of organic matter are available at most garden centers and your county extension office. For a more thorough analysis, soil samples can be sent to special testing facilities. Use the recommendations from your soil test to guide you in making any necessary soil adjustments.

Microclimates are small areas that are generally warmer or colder than the surrounding area. Buildings, fences, trees and other large objects can provide extra shelter in winter, but they may trap heat in summer, thereby creating a warmer microclimate. The bottoms of hills are usually colder than the tops, but often with less wind. Take advantage of these special areas when you plan your garden and choose your plants. In a warm,

Hardiness Zones Map

Average Annual Minimum Temperature	
6a	-5 to -10
6b	0 to -5
7a	5 to 0
7b	10 to 5

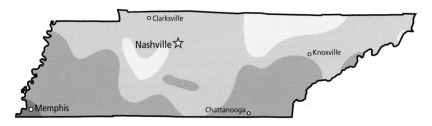

sheltered location, you may be able to successfully grow out-of-zone plants.

Selecting Plants

It's important to purchase healthy, pest-free, disease-free plants. Such plants establish quickly and won't introduce problems that may spread to other plants. You should have a good idea of what the plant is supposed to look like—the color and shape of the leaves and the habit of the plant—and then inspect the plant for signs of disease or pest infestation.

Most plants for sale are container-grown. Containers are an efficient way for nurseries and greenhouses to grow plants, but a plant grown in a restricted space for too long can become pot bound, with its roots densely encircling the inside of the pot. Avoid purchasing root-bound plants, because they are often stressed and can take longer to establish or may not establish at all. You can often temporarily remove the pot to examine the roots. At the same time, check for soil-borne insects and rotten roots. Healthy roots are white to light brown in color.

Planting Basics

The following tips apply to all plants:

• Pick the season for the best establishment of new plants. Trees and shrubs can be planted year-round in Tennessee, but November through February is ideal, because the plants are dormant, water is usually plentiful, and new roots quickly establish the plant when spring comes. Carefully monitor the water needs of plants planted in late spring or summer, because heat and drought stress can be fatal. Perennials establish best in September or early spring. The more time annuals have before the heat of the summer, the better they perform.

• Know the mature size. Place your plants based on their size at maturity rather than how big they are when you plant them. Large plants should have enough room to mature without interfering with walls, roof overhangs, power lines and walkways.

• Prepare the garden before planting. Dig or till the soil, pull up any weeds and make any needed amendments before you begin planting, if possible. These preparations may be more difficult in established beds to which you want to add a single plant. The prepared area should be at least twice the size of the plant you want to put in, and preferably the expected size of the mature plant's root system.

• Accommodate the rootball. If you prepared your planting spot ahead of time, your planting hole needs to be only big enough to accommodate the root ball with the roots spread out slightly.

Gently remove container.

Ensure proper planting depth.

Backfill with soil.

- Unwrap the roots. To allow the roots to spread out naturally, it is always best to remove any container before planting. In particular, you should remove plastic containers, fiber pots, wire and burlap before planting trees. Fiber pots decompose very slowly, if at all, and wick moisture away from the plant. Synthetic burlap won't decompose, and wire can strangle the roots as they mature. The only exceptions to this rule are peat pots and pellets used to start annuals and vegetables; they decompose and can be planted with the young transplants.

- Plant at the same depth in the soil. Plants generally like to grow at a specific level in relation to the soil and should be planted at the same level they were growing at before you transplanted them.

- Settle the soil with water. Good contact between the roots and the soil is important, but pressing the soil down too firmly, as often happens when you step on it, can cause compaction, which reduces the movement of water through the soil and leaves very few air spaces. Instead, pour water in as you fill the hole with soil. The water will settle the soil evenly without allowing it to compact.

- Identify your plants. Keep track of what's what by putting a tag next to each plant when you plant it or recording plant names and locations on a key and sketch of your garden. Over time, it is very easy to forget exactly what you planted and where.

- Water frequently. Be sure to water new plants frequently for 1–2 weeks, until they begin to get established. Always check the root zone before you water. More gardeners overwater than underwater. Once plants get established, water deeply and infrequently. Deep watering forces the roots to grow as they search for water, thereby helping the plants survive dry spells.

Annuals

Annuals are planted new each year and are expected to last only for a single growing season. Their flowers and decorative foliage provide bright splashes of color and can fill in spaces around immature trees, shrubs and perennials.

Annuals are easy to plant and are usually sold in small packs of four or six. The roots quickly fill the space in these small packs, so the small rootball should be broken up before planting. For most annuals, split the ball in two up the center or run your thumb up each side to break up the roots.

Many annuals are grown from seed. Plants that dislike their roots being disturbed do best when sown in place or grown in peat pots or pellets to minimize root disturbance.

Settle backfilled soil with water.   Water the plant well.   Add a layer of mulch.

Winter annuals can be planted in late fall or early winter. Summer annuals can be planted in spring. Be aware of your local frost dates, because some summer annuals are quite tender.

Perennials

Perennials grow for three or more years. They usually die back to the ground each fall and send up new shoots in spring, although some are evergreen. They often have a shorter period of bloom than annuals but require less care.

Many perennials benefit from being divided every few years. Doing so keeps them growing and blooming vigorously and is often helpful to control their spread. Dividing involves digging the plant up, removing dead bits, breaking or cutting the plant into several pieces and replanting some or all of them. Extra pieces can become gifts for family, friends and neighbors.

Trees & Shrubs

Trees and shrubs provide the bones of the garden. They are often the slowest growing plants but usually the longest lived. They may be characterized by deciduous or evergreen leaf type, and may be broad-leaved or needled.

Trees should have as little disturbed soil as possible at the bottom of the planting

Roses are lovely on their own or in mixed borders.

hole. Loose dirt settles over time, and sinking even an inch can kill some trees.

Staking, sometimes recommended for newly planted trees, is necessary only for trees over 5' tall.

Pruning is more often required for shrubs than trees. It helps them maintain an attractive shape and can improve blooming. If you have never pruned before, it is a good idea to take a pruning course or to hire or consult with an ISA (International Society of Arboriculture) certified arborist.

Roses

Roses are beautiful shrubs with lovely, often-fragrant blooms. Traditionally, most roses bloomed only once per year, but most new varieties bloom for much or all of summer.

Generally, roses prefer a fertile, well-prepared planting area, although many roses are quite durable and adapt to poorer conditions. As a guide, prepare an area 24" long, 24" wide and 24" deep. Add plenty of compost or other fertile organic matter. Keep roses well watered during the growing season. Like all shrubs, roses have specific pruning requirements.

Trees and shrubs provide backbone to the mixed border.

Training vines to climb arbors adds structure to the garden.

Lilies bloom throughout the summer.

Vines

Vines or climbing plants are useful for screening and shade, especially where a tree won't fit. They may be woody or herbaceous and annual or perennial.

Most vines need sturdy support, such as a trellis, arbor, porch railing, fence, wall, pole or tree. To avoid disturbing the vine's roots, install any necessary supports before planting.

Bulbs

Some popular plants have fleshy underground storage organs that allow them to survive extended periods of dormancy. They are often grown for the bright splashes of color their flowers provide. They may flower in spring, summer or fall.

Hardy selections can be left in the ground to flower every year. The bulbs, corms or tubers of tender plants are generally lifted from the garden as the foliage dies back in fall, then stored in a cool, frost-free location until replanting in spring.

Herbs

Herbs may be medicinal, culinary or both. A few common culinary herbs are listed in this book. Even if you don't cook with them, the often-fragrant foliage adds its aroma to the garden, and the plants have decorative forms, leaves and flowers.

Many herbs have flowers that attract butterflies, bees and hummingbirds. They also attract predatory insects, which help to manage pest problems by feasting on problem insects such as aphids, mealy bugs and whiteflies.

Ferns Grasses & Groundcovers

Foliage is an important consideration when choosing plants. Although many plants look spectacular in bloom, they can seem dull without flowers. Including a variety of plants with interesting or striking foliage in your garden can provide all the color and texture you want without relying on flowers.

Ornamental grasses make great garden additions. They offer a variety of textures and foliage colors, providing at least three seasons of interest. There is an ornamental grass for every garden situation and condition, from hot and dry to cool and wet, and for any type of soil.

Herbs are useful and attractive garden plants.

Ornamental grasses have few insect or disease problems. Other than cutting back perennial species in fall or spring, little maintenance is required. Be aware that dried grass is highly flammable. Left standing for winter interest, it can be a fire hazard, so cut grasses near houses and other structures back in fall.

Ferns are ancient plants that have adapted to many different environments. This large group of plants offers interesting foliage in a wide array of shapes and colors. Instead of producing flowers,

Ornamental grasses add color, variety and texture.

ferns reproduce by spores borne in structures on the undersides and margins of the foliage. Ferns generally favor moist, shaded gardens, but some thrive in the dry, deep shade of trees such as magnolias.

Many plants classified as annuals, perennials, trees, shrubs, vines or herbs also have wonderful foliage and will be an asset to your garden landscape.

Spreading plants with dense growth are often used to control soil erosion, keep weeds at bay and fill garden areas that are difficult to maintain.

Groundcovers can be herbaceous or woody and annual or perennial. Aggressive vines make excellent groundcovers, but any densely growing plant that covers the ground can be used. Suitable plants are distributed throughout this book. Small plants or ones with a slow spread need to be placed sufficiently close together to be effective.

Final Comments

We encourage you to visit the outstanding garden shows, county fairs, public gardens, arboretums and private gardens (get permission first) we have here in Tennessee to see which plants grow best and which ones catch your interest. A walk through your neighborhood is also a grand way to see which plants might do well in your own garden. Don't be afraid to ask questions.

Also, don't be afraid to experiment. No matter how many books you read, trying things yourself is the best way to learn and to find out what will grow in your garden. Remember that a great garden is dynamic, changing from season to season and year to year, rather than static. Great gardens evolve. Use the information provided as guidelines, and have fun!

Ageratum • Floss Flower

Ageratum

A. houstonianum 'Hawaii Blue' (above), A. houstonianum (below)

Ageratum's fluffy flowers, often in shades of blue, add softness and texture to the garden.

Growing

Ageratum prefers **full sun** but tolerates partial shade. The soil should be **fertile, moist** and **well drained**. A moisture-retaining mulch prevents the soil from drying out excessively. Deadhead to prolong blooming and to keep the plant looking tidy.

Tips

The small selections, which become almost completely covered in flowers, make excellent edging plants for flowerbeds and are attractive when grouped in masses or grown in planters. The tall selections can be included in the center of a flowerbed and are useful as cut flowers.

Recommended

*A. **houstonianum*** forms a large, leggy mound that can grow up to 24" tall, although many cultivars have been developed that have a low, bushy habit and generally grow about 12" tall. Flowers are produced in shades of blue, purple, pink or white.

Features: fuzzy blue, purple, pink or white flowers; mounded habit **Height:** 6–36"
Spread: 6–18"

Begonia
Begonia

Whether you want beautiful flowers, a compact habit or decorative foliage, begonias are sure to fulfill your shade-gardening needs.

Growing
Begonias prefer **light or partial shade** and **fertile, neutral to acidic, well-drained** soil **rich in organic matter**. Some wax begonias tolerate sun if their soil is kept moist. Allow the soil to dry out slightly between waterings, particularly for tuberous begonias. Plant begonias only once the soil has warmed. In cold soil, they may become stunted and fail to thrive.

Tips
Plant trailing tuberous begonias in hanging baskets and along rock walls. Wax begonias make attractive edging plants. Rex begonias are useful as specimen plants in containers and beds.

Recommended
B. **Rex Cultorum Hybrids** (rex begonias) are grown for their dramatic, colorful foliage.

B. semperflorens (wax begonias) have a neat, rounded habit combined with pink, white, red or bicolored flowers and green, bronze, reddish or white-variegated foliage. Bronze foliage selections tolerate full sun.

B. x *tuberhybrida* (tuberous begonias) are generally sold as tubers. Their flowers bloom in many shades of red, pink, yellow, orange or white.

B. Rex Cultorum Hybrids 'Escargot' (above)
B. x *tuberhybrida* (below)

To avoid tuber rot in tuberous begonias, water along the edge of containers or around the dripline of in-ground plants—never water near the stem. Also, keep the mildew-prone foliage dry.

Features: pink, white, red, yellow, orange, bicolored or picotee flowers; decorative foliage
Height: 6–24" **Spread:** 6–24"

Butter Daisy
Melampodium

𝒯his Southern favorite is adored for its bright sunny flowers and growth habit—and for its tolerance for extreme heat and humidity, which stops it from melting down even in mid-summer.

Growing
Butter daisy prefers **full sun** or **partial shade**. The soil should be of **average fertility, well drained** and amended with **compost**. Keep the soil moist until the plants are established but then begin to let it dry out between waterings to build the drought tolerance needed for the heat of summer. Butter daisy prefers not to be fertilized too frequently.

Tips
Butter daisy is ideal for planting en masse in flowerbeds for maximum impact. Using fewer plants than you might expect, it fills and spreads to cover an area without becoming invasive. The dwarf varieties are nicely suited to containers and mix well with an assortment of other annuals and perennials.

This 'self-cleaning' annual sheds its spent flowers on a regular basis and doesn't require pinching to encourage branching. Let it be and watch it thrive. It easily reseeds, so watch for volunteer plants each summer.

M. paludosum 'Showstar' (above)
M. paludosum (below)

Recommended
M. paludosum produces masses of short-stemmed, starry-shaped, bright yellow flowers above narrow, dark green leaves. A number of cultivars are available. **'Lemon Delight'** is a dwarf cultivar, and **'Million Gold'** is an exceptional selection that remains small in size. **'Showstar'** grows twice as big as the dwarf selections.

Features: bright yellow flowers; attractive habit; drought tolerance **Height:** 10–24"
Spread: 12–24"

Celosia
Celosia

C. argentea Plumosa Group (above), *C. argentea* Cristata Group (below)

The unusual wrinkled texture of celosia's flowers and the incredible variety of flower forms will make any gardener crow with delight.

Growing
Celosia prefers **full sun** and tolerates summer heat. The soil should be **fertile** and **well drained,** with plenty of **organic matter** worked in. Celosias like to be watered regularly.

This plant does not require deadheading. Pinching out the first flower bloom, however, results in fuller plants with many more blooms.

Tips
Use celosia in borders and beds as well as in planters. The flowers make interesting additions to cut arrangements, either fresh or dried. A mass planting of plume celosia looks bright and cheerful. The popular crested varieties work well as accents.

Recommended
C. argentea is the parent of the many crested and plume-type varieties and cultivars now available, but the species itself is never grown. **Cristata Group** (crested celosia) has blooms that resemble brains or rooster combs in bright, vivid colors. **Plumosa Group** (plume celosia) has feathery, plume-like blooms in deep, rich colors.

To dry celosia plumes, pick the flowers when they are at their peak and hang them upside down in a cool, shaded place.

Features: red, orange, gold, yellow, pink or purple flowers **Height:** 10–36"
Spread: 10–36"

Coleus
Solenostemon (Coleus)

There is a coleus for everyone. With foliage from brash yellows, oranges and reds to deep maroon and rose selections, the colors, textures and variations of coleus are almost limitless.

Growing

Coleus has traditionally been a shade plant, but the vast majority of selections sold today like **full sun**. The soil should be of **rich to average fertility, humus rich, moist** and **well drained**.

Tips

The bold, colorful foliage makes a dramatic impact when the plants are grouped together as edging plants or in beds, borders or mixed containers. Select colors to complement bold-flowered companion plants. Coleus can also be grown indoors as a house-plant in a bright room.

Coleus tends to stretch out and become less attractive after flowering. Prevention is as simple as pinching off the flower buds as they develop.

Recommended

S. scutellarioides (*Coleus blumei* var. *verschaffeltii*) forms a bushy mound of foliage. The leaf edges range from slightly toothed to very ruffled. The leaves are usually multi-colored, with shades ranging from pale greenish yellow to deep purple-black. Dozens of cultivars are available.

S. scutellarioides Wizard Series (above)
S. scutellarioides cultivars (below)

Coleus can be trained to grow into a standard (tree) form by pinching off the side branches as the plant grows. Once the plant reaches the desired height, pinch from the top to encourage bushy growth.

Features: brightly colored foliage; insignificant purple flowers **Height:** 6–36"
Spread: usually equal to height

Dusty Miller
Senecio

S. cineraria 'Silver Dust' (above), *S. cineraria* (below)

Dusty miller makes a great addition to planters, window boxes and mixed borders. The soft, silvery gray, deeply lobed foliage makes a good backdrop for the brightly colored flowers of other annuals.

Growing
Dusty miller grows well in **full sun** or **partial shade**. The soil should be of **average fertility** and **well drained**.

Tips
This plant's soft, silvery, lacy foliage is its main feature. Used primarily as an edging plant, dusty miller is also suitable for beds, borders and containers.

The flowers aren't showy, so most people pinch them off the before they bloom to stop them from using energy that would otherwise go to producing more foliage.

Dusty miller is a hardy annual in Tennessee. It is common to see it overwinter and perform year-round.

Recommended
S. cineraria forms a mound of fuzzy, silvery gray, lobed or finely divided foliage. Many cultivars with impressive foliage colors and shapes have been developed.

When cut for fresh- or dried-flower arrangements, dusty miller makes a wonderful filler that adds a lacy texture.

Features: silvery foliage; neat habit; yellow to cream flowers **Height:** 12–24"
Spread: equal to height or slightly narrower

Flowering Cabbage Ornamental Kale

Brassica

*W*ith its stunning variegated foliage, flowering cabbage is wonderful in containers and flower boxes.

Growing

Flowering cabbage prefers **full sun** but tolerates partial shade. The soil should be **neutral to slightly alkaline, fertile, well drained** and **moist**. For best results, fertilize several times through winter.

In Tennessee, this plant is best used as a winter annual. It performs best from September to March. Its colors brighten after a light frost or when the air temperature drops below 50° F.

Tips

Flowering cabbage plants can be started in trays and transplanted in fall. Many packages of seeds contain a variety of cultivars.

Wait until some true leaves develop before thinning. Use the unneeded leaves in salads.

This tough, bold plant is at home in both vegetable gardens and flowerbeds. It makes a dramatic show when used en masse or in combination with other winter annuals such as pansies and snapdragons.

To extend the visual appeal of flowering cabbage, remove the flowers when they first appear.

Recommended

B. oleracea (**Acephala Group**) forms loose, erect rosettes of large, often-fringed leaves in shades of purple, red, pink and white. It grows 12–24" tall, with an equal spread. **Osaka series** plants grow 12" tall and wide, with wavy foliage that is red to pink in the center and blue to green near the edge.

Features: colorful, edible foliage
Height: 12–24" **Spread:** 12–24"

Impatiens
Impatiens

I. walleriana (above), *I. hawkeri* (below)

Impatiens are the high-wattage darlings of the shade garden, delivering masses of flowers in a wide variety of colors.

Growing

Impatiens do best in **partial shade** or **light shade** but can tolerate full shade. The soil should be **fertile, humus rich, moist** and **well drained**. In Tennessee, New Guinea impatiens does best with morning sun and afternoon shade.

Tips

Impatiens are known for their ability to grow and flower profusely, even in shade. Mass plant them in beds under trees, along shady fences or walls, or in porch planters. They also look lovely in hanging baskets. New Guinea impatiens is grown as much for its variegated leaves as for its flowers.

Recommended

I. hawkeri (New Guinea hybrids, New Guinea impatiens) flowers in shades of red, orange, pink, purple or white. The foliage is often variegated with a yellow stripe down the center of each leaf. Many cultivars are available in various flower and foliage colors.

I. walleriana (impatiens, busy Lizzie) flowers in shades of purple, red, burgundy, pink, yellow, salmon, orange, apricot or white and can be bicolored. Dozens of cultivars are available.

New impatiens varieties are introduced every year, expanding the selection of sizes, forms and colors for our gardens.

Features: flowers in shades of purple, red, burgundy, pink, yellow, salmon, orange, apricot, white or bicolored; flowers well in shade **Height:** 6–36" **Spread:** 12–24"

Lantana

Lantana

This low-maintenance plant, with its stunning flowers, thrives in hot weather and won't suffer if you forget to water it.

Growing

Lantana grows best in **full sun** but tolerates partial shade. The soil should be **fertile, moist** and **well drained**. Lantana tolerates heat and drought. This 'self-cleaning' plant doesn't require deadheading.

Tips

Lantana is a tender shrub that is grown as an annual. It is an attractive addition to beds and borders, or in mixed containers and hanging baskets.

Recommended

L. camara is a bushy plant that bears round clusters of flowers in a variety of colors. The flowers often change color as they mature, giving the clusters a striking, multi-colored appearance. Good examples of this effect are **'Feston Rose,'** which has flowers that open yellow and mature to bright pink, and **'Radiation,'** which bears flowers that open yellow and mature to red.

L. camara cultivar (above)
L. camara 'Radiation' (below)

A shrubby annual, lantana grows quickly to make a striking addition to mixed planters, combining well with other heat-tolerant annuals.

Features: stunning flowers in yellow, orange, pink, purple, red or white, often in combination
Height: 18–24" **Spread:** up to 4'

Madagascar Periwinkle
Catharanthus

C. roseus (above & below)

Madagascar periwinkle is a forgiving annual that tolerates dry spells, searing sun and city pollution. It exhibits grace under all sorts of pressure.

Growing
Madagascar periwinkle prefers **full sun** but tolerates partial shade. Any **well-drained** soil is fine. This plant tolerates pollution and drought but prefers to be watered regularly. It doesn't like to be too wet or too cold, so wait until the soil has warmed before planting it. This 'self-cleaning' plant requires no deadheading.

Tips
Madagascar periwinkle does best in the sunniest, warmest part of the garden. Plant it in a bed along an exposed driveway or against the south-facing wall of the house. It can also be used in hanging baskets, in planters and as a temporary groundcover.

Recommended
C. roseus (*Vinca rosea*) forms a mound of strong stems. The flowers are pink, red or white, often with contrasting centers. Many cultivars are available, including the **Pacifica series,** with flowers in lilac, pale pink or white, and the early-blooming **Tropicana series,** with very large, rounded flowers.

One of the best annuals to use in front of homes on busy streets, Madagascar periwinkle will bloom happily despite exposure to exhaust fumes and dust.

Features: attractive foliage; flowers in shades of red, pink, white or purple, often with contrasting centers; durability
Height: 6–24" **Spread:** usually equal to or greater than height

Mexican Sunflower

Tithonia

For that 'hot' look in your garden, Mexican sunflower is one of the best plants you can grow.

Growing

Full sun is best. The soil should be of **average to poor fertility, moist** and **well drained**. This 'self-cleaning' annual requires no deadheading.

Some selections grow quite large, so make sure you read the labels and space the plants appropriately.

Tips

Heat-resistant Mexican sunflower is ideal for growing in a sunny, warm spot. Some tall selections break easily if exposed to too much wind; grow them along a wall or fence to provide shelter and stability. These coarse-looking annuals are well suited to the back of a border as a good backdrop to a bed of shorter annuals.

Recommended

T. rotundifolia is a vigorous, bushy plant with vibrant orange flowers. **'Fiesta del Sol,'** the first dwarf *Tithonia* cultivar available on the market, was designated as an All-American Selection in 1968. It bears deep orange flowers on 24–30" tall plants. **'Goldfinger'** is taller than the species and bears large, orange flowers. **'Torch'** has bright red-orange flowers.

T. rotundifolia (above & below)

It's not surprising, given its love of heat and fiery colors, that this annual hails from parts of Mexico and Central America.

Features: orange, red-orange or yellow-orange flowers; tolerates heat and humidity
Height: 2–4' **Spread:** 24–30"

Nasturtium

Tropaeolum

T. majus (above), T. majus 'Alaska' (below)

Combine nasturtiums with vegetables and other ornamental edible plants in containers and window boxes. The edible leaves and flowers add a peppery flavor to salads.

This fast-growing, brightly colored flower is easy to grow, making it popular with beginners and experienced gardeners alike.

Growing

Nasturtium prefers **full sun** but tolerates some shade and likes things a bit **cool**. The soil should be of **poor to average fertility, light, moist** and **well drained**. Plants grown in fertile soil produce many leaves and few flowers. Let the soil drain completely between waterings.

Tips

Nasturtium is used in beds, borders and containers. It thrives in poor locations. Combine it with other winter annuals, such as flowering cabbage.

Recommended

T. *majus* has a trailing habit, but many of its cultivars have bushier, more refined habits, and they offer a range of flower colors and variegated foliage.

Features: bright, edible flowers in red, orange, yellow, burgundy, pink, cream, gold, white or bicolored; attractive, edible leaves; varied habits **Height:** 12–18" for dwarf varieties; up to 10' for trailing varieties **Spread:** equal to height

Ornamental Pepper
Capsicum

*I*t's not always necessary to rely on the beauty of the flowers when planting annuals. Ornamental pepper with the colorful fruit is what will catch everyone's attention.

Growing
Ornamental pepper likes **full sun**. The soil should be **fertile, moist, well drained** and **rich with organic amendments** such as compost. Don't let the soil dry out, causing the plants to wilt—the result will be stunted growth and little or no fruit.

Wait until the soil has warmed and the risk of frost has passed before planting out the seedlings.

Tips
Ornamental peppers work well in mixed borders and decorative containers. Choose companions with flower and foliage colors complementary to the pepper's fruit color. For maximum impact, plant peppers in groups or en masse, because single specimens tend to 'get lost' amid the other plants.

Recommended
C. annuum closely resembles plants grown strictly for fruit but is often slightly smaller. Inconspicuous white or yellow summer flowers are followed by shiny, conical fruit. The fruits emerge in pale cream and yellow but slowly mature into shades of purple,

C. annuum cultivar

orange, yellow or red. The many cultivars offer variegated foliage and spherical fruit in varied colors. **'Explosive Ember'** is a new cultivar bearing deep, dark purple foliage and fruit which matures to a bright red.

Ornamental pepper is the perfect edible addition to any sunny setting. The colorful fruit can be dried and used in crafts and arrangements.

Features: colorful, shiny, waxy, edible (possibly hot) fruit; attractive habit
Height: 6–36" **Spread:** 6–24"

Pansy
Viola

V. x wittrockiana (above), *V. tricolor* (below)

Pansies are among the most popular winter annuals available, and for good reason. They love our Tennessee winter temperatures and make a great landscape show from September to March.

Growing
Pansies prefer **full sun** but tolerate partial shade. The soil should be **fertile**, **moist** and **well drained**.

Tips
Pansies can be used in beds and borders or mixed with spring-flowering bulbs. They can also be grown in containers. With the varied color combinations available, pansies complement other winter annuals such as flowering cabbage, red mustard, nasturtium and snapdragon.

For a dramatic show, space pansies about 6–8" apart.

Recommended
V. tricolor (Johnny-jump-up) bears flowers in shades of purple, lavender blue, white or yellow, with dark purple upper petals. The lower petals are usually streaked with dark purple. The many cultivars offer larger flowers in various colors.

V. x wittrockiana is available in a wide variety of solid, patterned, bicolored and multi-colored flowers with face-like markings, in every size imaginable. The bright green foliage is lightly scalloped along the edges.

The more you pick, the more profusely the plants bloom, so deadhead throughout winter.

Features: blue, purple, red, orange, yellow, pink, white or multi-colored flowers
Height: 3–10" **Spread:** 6–12"

Persian Shield

Strobilanthes

S. dyerianus (above & below)

Persian shield's iridescent foliage in shades of purple, bronze, silver and pink adds a bright touch to any annual planting.

Growing

Persian shield grows well in **full sun or partial shade**. The soil should be **average to fertile, light** and **very well drained**. Pinch the growing tips to encourage bushy growth. Cuttings can be started in late summer and overwintered indoors.

Tips

The colorful foliage provides a dramatic background in annual or mixed beds and borders and in container plantings. Combine with yellow- or white-flowered plants for stunning contrast or with complementary lavender-flowered plants.

Recommended

S. dyerianus forms a mound of silver- or purple-flushed foliage with contrasting dark green, bronze or purple veins and margins. Spikes of blue flowers may appear in early fall.

Persian shield can be overwintered in a cool, bright location indoors.

Features: decorative foliage; blue flowers
Height: 18–36" **Spread:** 24–36"

Petunia

Petunia

Milliflora type 'Fantasy' (above), Multiflora type (below)

For speedy growth, prolific blooming, ease of care and a huge variety of selections, petunia is hard to beat.

Growing
Petunia prefers **full sun**. The soil should be of **average to rich fertility, light, sandy** and **well drained**. Pinch halfway back in mid-summer to keep the plants bushy and to encourage new growth and flowers.

Tips
Use petunias in beds, borders, containers and hanging baskets.

Recommended
P. x hybrida is a large group of popular, sun-loving annuals that fall into three categories. **Grandifloras** have the largest (but fewest) flowers in the widest range of colors, but they can be damaged by rain. **Millifloras** have the smallest flowers in the narrowest range of colors, but this type is the most prolific and least likely to be damaged by heavy rain. **Multifloras** bear intermediate sizes and numbers of flowers and suffer intermediate rain damage. Cultivars of all types are available, and new selections are made available almost every year.

The rekindling of interest in petunias resulted largely from the development of exciting new selections, such as the Supertunia hybrids and Wave Series of petunias. These continuously blooming, vigorously spreading, dense-growing hybrids tolerate wet weather and offer tremendous options for hanging baskets, containers and borders.

Features: flowers in every color in solid, bicolor or multi-color; versatility **Height:** 6–18" **Spread:** 12–24" or wider

Rose Moss
Portulaca

*F*or a brilliant show in the hottest, driest, most neglected area of the garden, you can't go wrong with rose moss.

Growing
Rose moss requires **full sun**. The soil should be of **poor fertility, sandy and well drained**. If you sow directly outdoors, rain may transport the tiny seeds to unexpected places. To ensure that you have plants where you want them, start the seed indoors. Rose moss also self-seeds, often providing a colorful show year after year.

Tips
Rose moss grows well under the eaves of a house or in a dry, rocky, exposed area. It also makes a great addition to a hanging basket on a sunny front porch. Remember to water it occasionally. As long as the location is sunny, this plant does well with minimal care.

Recommended
P. grandiflora forms a bushy mound of succulent foliage. It bears delicate, papery, rose-like flowers profusely all summer. Many cultivars are available, including ones with flowers that stay open on cloudy days.

P. grandiflora (above & below)

Rose moss plants can be placed close together and allowed to intertwine for an interesting and attractive effect.

Features: drought-resistant summer flowers in shades of red, pink, yellow, white, purple, orange or peach **Height:** 4–8"
Spread: 6–12" or wider

Salvia

Salvia

S. *splendens* (above), S. *viridis* (below)

Salvias should be part of every annual garden—the attractive and varied forms have something to offer any style of garden.

With over 900 species of Salvia to choose from, you're sure to find one you'll like for your garden.

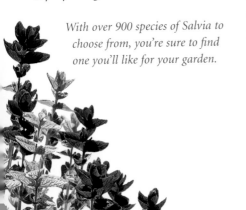

Growing

Salvias prefer **full sun** but tolerate light shade. The soil should be **moist, well drained** and of **average to rich fertility**, with a lot of **organic matter**.

Tips

Salvias look good grouped in beds and borders and in containers. The long-lasting flowers make good cut flowers for arrangements.

To keep the plants producing flowers, water often and fertilize monthly.

Recommended

S. argentea (silver sage) is grown for its large, fuzzy, silvery leaves.

S. coccinea (Texas sage) is a bushy, upright plant that bears whorled spikes of white, pink, blue or purple flowers.

S. farinacea (mealy cup sage, blue sage) has bright blue flowers clustered along stems powdered with silver. Cultivars are available.

S. splendens (salvia, scarlet sage) is grown for its spikes of tubular, bright red flowers. Recently, cultivars have become available in white, pink, purple or orange.

S. viridis (*S. horminium;* annual clary sage) is grown for its colorful pink, purple, blue or white bracts, not for its flowers.

Features: red, blue, purple, pink, orange, yellow, cream, white or bicolored summer flowers or bracts; attractive foliage
Height: 8"–4' **Spread:** 8"–4'

Snapdragon
Antirrhinum

Snapdragon is a great winter annual in Tennessee. The flower colors are always rich and vibrant, and even the most jaded gardeners are tempted to squeeze open the dragons' mouths. Snapdragon doesn't like our summer heat, however, so use it for a fall-to-spring show.

Growing

Snapdragon prefers **full sun** but tolerates light or partial shade. The soil should be **fertile, rich in organic matter, neutral to alkaline** and **well drained**. This plant doesn't perform well in acidic soil.

For bushier growth, pinch the tips of the young plants. To promote further blooming and to prevent the plant from dying back before the end of the season, cut off the flower spikes as they fade.

Tips

The height of the variety dictates the best place for it in a border—the shortest varieties work well near the front, and the tallest look good in the back. The dwarf and medium-height varieties can be used in planters. Trailing varieties do well in hanging baskets.

Recommended

A. majus has been developed into many cultivars. They are generally grouped into three size categories: dwarf, medium and giant.

A. majus cultivars (above & below)

Combine snapdragons with other winter annuals or interplant them with spring-flowering bulbs. Mulch well with pine-needle mulch for added winter protection.

Features: white, cream, yellow, orange, red, maroon, pink, purple or bicolored summer flowers **Height:** 6"–4' **Spread:** 6–24"

Spreading Zinnia
Zinnia

Z. haageana 'Orange Star' (above)
Z. angustifolia cultivar (below)

Spreading zinnias are great die-hard annuals that take summer heat and sun extremely well. Unlike *Z. elegans*, the old-fashioned cut-flower type, spreading zinnia is disease resistant.

Growing
Spreading zinnias grow best in **full sun**. The soil should be **fertile, rich in organic matter, moist** and **well drained**. These 'self-cleaning' plants require no deadheading or pinching.

Tips
Spreading zinnias are useful in beds, borders and containers.

Recommended
Z. angustifolia (spreading zinnia, narrow-leaf zinnia) is a low, mounding, mildew-resistant plant that bears yellow, orange or white flowers. It grows up to about 8" tall. The cultivars available include the **Profusion series,** with flowers in shades of pink, orange or white.

Z. haageana (Mexican zinnia) is a bushy plant with narrow, mildew-resistant leaves that bears bright bicolored or tricolored, daisy-like flowers in shades of orange, red, yellow, maroon, brown or gold. It grows 12–24" tall. Cultivars are available.

All zinnias are great for attracting butterflies.

Features: bushy; flowers in shades of red, yellow, orange, pink, white, maroon, brown, gold, bicolored or tricolored **Height:** 8–36"
Spread: 12"

Sunflower
Helianthus

The image of sunflowers alongside a weathered barn or tall garden shed has inspired artists of all ages throughout history.

Growing
Annual sunflower grows best in **full sun**. The soil should be of **average fertility, humus rich, moist** and **well drained**.

Annual sunflower is an excellent plant for children to grow. Big and easy to handle, the seeds germinate quickly.

To ensure flowers until frost, stagger the sowing of sunflowers 2 weeks apart from early spring until July, because the flowers last only 4–6 weeks.

Tips
The low-growing varieties can be used in beds and borders. The tall varieties are effective at the backs of borders and make good screens and temporary hedges. The tallest varieties may need staking.

Carefree gardeners let sunflowers go to seed right in the garden to produce new blooms the following summer.

Recommended
H. annuus (common sunflower) is considered weedy, but many attractive new cultivars have been developed.

H. annuus cultivars (above & below)

Birds flock to the ripening seedheads of sunflowers and quickly pluck out the tightly packed seeds.

Features: most commonly yellow, but also orange, red, brown, cream or bicolored flowers, typically with brown, purple or rusty red centers; edible seeds **Height:** 24" for dwarf varieties; up to 15' for giants **Spread:** 12–24"

Trailing Petunia • Million Bells

Calibrachoa

Calibrachoa 'Trailing Pink' (above & below)

Given the right conditions, the charming trailing petunia will bloom continuously during the growing season.

Growing

Trailing petunia prefers **full sun**. The soil should be **fertile, moist** and **well drained**. Although it prefers to be watered regularly, trailing petunia is fairly drought resistant once established.

Tips

Popular for planters and hanging baskets, trailing petunia is also attractive in beds and borders. It grows all summer and needs plenty of room to spread, or it will overtake other flowers. Pinch back to keep the plants compact.

Recommended

Calibrachoa **hybrids** have a dense, trailing habit. They bear small flowers that look like regular petunias. The **Superbells series** is noted for superior disease resistance and a wide range of flower colors.

Trailing petunia blooms well into fall; it becomes hardier over summer and as the weather cools.

Features: pink, purple, yellow, red-orange, white or blue flowers; trailing habit **Height:** 6–12" **Spread:** up to 24"

Verbena

Verbena

Verbenas are open, airy plants that will attract a plethora of butterflies.

Growing

Verbenas grow best in **full sun**. The soil should be of average **fertility** and **very well drained**. Established verbenas tolerate drought. Cut or pinch the plants back by one-half in mid-summer to encourage more fall blooms. Verbenas self-seed in abundance, but the seedlings are easy to control.

Tips

Use verbenas in the front or middle of beds and borders, and to add height to containers. Because verbenas look so wispy when in flower, they look best when mass planted.

Most verbenas are tender or short-lived perennials that are treated as annuals.

Recommended

V. bonariensis forms a low clump of foliage. Tall, stiff, airy stems bear clusters of small, purple flowers.

V. canadensis (rose verbena) bears rosy-purple flowers atop a compact form that grows 18" tall and 18–36" wide. The cultivars available include **'Greystone Daphne,'** which bears lavender pink flowers, and **'Homestead Purple,'** which has dark purple flowers and glossy foliage.

V. caradensis 'Greystone Daphne' (above)
V. x hybrida (below)

V. x hybrida (garden verbena) is densely branched, with grayish green foliage and compact flower clusters in solid white, pink, bright red, purple or blue or combinations.

V. rigida (vervain) is an erect to spreading plant 18–24" tall and 16" wide, with stalkless, toothed, coarsely textured, hairy leaves and fragrant, purple or magenta summer flowers. Cultivars are available with red, violet blue or silvery blue flowers.

In humid summers, verbena is prone to powdery mildew. Usually, overall plant health and flowering are unaffected, but severe outbreaks can really weaken a plant.

Features: early- to late-summer flowers in purple, red, white, pink, peach, blue, violet blue or silvery blue; attractive habit
Height: 18"–6' **Spread:** 12–24"
Hardiness: zones 6–9

Wishbone Flower

Torenia

T. fournieri cultivars (above & below)

Wishbone flower comes in several deeply colored cultivars, and it is the perfect plant to point out to children, who are often intrigued by familiar shapes showing up in strange places.

Growing

Wishbone flower grows well in either **full sun** or **light shade**. The soil should be **fertile, light, humus rich** and **moist**. This plant requires regular watering.

Don't cover the seeds when planting, because they require light to germinate.

Tips

Wishbone flower is very soothing and subtle, and it blends well in a garden. It can be massed in a bed or border, used as an edging plant or added to mixed containers and hanging baskets.

Recommended

T. fournieri is a bushy, rounded to upright plant. Its purple flowers have yellow throats. The **Clown series** features compact plants that flower in purple, blue, pink or white. **'Summer Wave Blue'** has a creeping habit and large, deep blue flowers.

The wishbone flower is named for the arrangements of its stamens (male parts) in the center of the flower.

Features: purple, pink, blue, white or bicolored flowers with a yellow spot on the lower petal **Height:** 6–12" **Spread:** 6–8"

Artemisia

Artemisia

Most artemisias are valued for their foliage, not their flowers. Silver is the ultimate blending color, because it enhances every hue placed next to it.

Growing

Artemisias grow best in **full sun,** in **well-drained** soil of **low to average fertility**. Rich soil causes lanky, invasive growth. Artemisias are very drought tolerant.

Artemisias respond well to pruning in late spring. If you prune before May, frost may kill any new growth. When artemisias look straggly, cut them back hard to encourage new growth and maintain a neater form. Divide them every year or two.

Tips

Use artemisias in rock gardens and borders. Their foliage makes a good backdrop for brightly colored flowers. Small forms may be used to create knot gardens.

Recommended

A variety of artemisias are available; check with your local garden center. Here are some favorites:

A. ludoviciana **cultivars** (white sage, silver sage) are vigorous, upright, clump-forming plants, hardy to zone 4.

A. ludoviciana 'Silver Queen' (above)
A. ludoviciana 'Valerie Finnis' (below)

A. **'Powis Castle'** is an outstanding mound-forming selection that produces delicate, ferny foliage in silvery tones, but no flowers.

A. stelleriana (beach wormwood) is a creeping groundcover selection with a dense habit and silvery gray foliage.

Also called: wormwood, sage
Features: silvery gray, feathery or deeply lobed foliage **Height:** 6"–6'
Spread: 12–36" **Hardiness:** zones 3–8

Aster

Aster (Symphyotrichum)

A. *novae-angliae* (above), A. *novi-belgii* (below)

Asters are among the final plants to bloom before the killing frosts arrive. Their purples and pinks contrast nicely with the yellow-flowered perennials common in the late-summer or fall garden.

Growing

Asters prefer **full sun** but tolerate partial shade. The soil should be **fertile, moist** and **well drained**.

Pinch or shear these plants back in early summer to promote dense growth and to reduce disease problems. Mulch in winter to protect the plants from temperature fluctuations. Divide every two or three years to maintain vigor and control spread.

Tips

Use asters in the middle of borders and in cottage-style gardens or naturalize them in wild gardens.

Recommended

Some *Aster* species have recently been reclassified under the genus *Symphyotrichum*. You may see both names at garden centers.

A. x *frikartii* (Frikart's aster) is an upright perennial with dark green, roughly textured leaves and light to dark violet blue flowers that emerge in late summer. This selection grows 24–36" tall and wide. Cultivars are available with lavender or blue flowers.

A. novae-angliae (Michaelmas daisy, New England aster) is an upright, spreading, clump-forming perennial that bears yellow-centered, purple flowers. Many cultivars are available.

A. novi-belgii (Michaelmas daisy, New York aster) is a dense, upright, clump-forming perennial with purple flowers. Many cultivars are available.

Features: late-summer to mid-fall flowers in shades of red, white, blue, purple, lavender or pink, often with yellow centers
Height: 10"–5' **Spread:** 18–36"
Hardiness: zones 3–8

Beebalm

Monarda

The fragrant flowers of this native plant are intoxicating to butterflies and bees—and to anyone who passes by.

Growing

Beebalm grows well in **full sun, partial shade** or **light shade** in **humus-rich, moist, well-drained** soil of **average fertility**. Dry conditions encourage mildew and loss of leaves. Divide every two or three years in spring, just as new growth emerges.

In June, cut back some of the stems by half to extend the flowering period and encourage compact growth. Thinning the stems in spring also helps prevent powdery mildew. If mildew strikes after flowering, cut the plants back to 6" to increase air circulation.

Tips

Use beebalm beside a stream or pond, or in a lightly shaded, well-watered border. It spreads in moist, fertile soils, but the shallow roots can be removed easily.

Beebalm attracts bees, butterflies and hummingbirds. Avoid using pesticides, which can seriously harm these creatures and make the plant unsuitable for culinary or medicinal purposes.

Recommended

M. didyma is a bushy, mounding plant that forms a thick clump of stems with red or pink flowers. Many cultivars are available, with varied colors, sizes and levels of mildew resistance.

Features: fragrant, red, pink or purple flowers **Height:** 2–4' **Spread:** 18–36" **Hardiness:** zones 3–8

M. didyma cultivar (above), *M. didyma* (below)

'Jacob Cline' produces deep red flowers and is resistant to powdery mildew.

M. fistulosa (bergamot) produces lavender to pale pink flowers surrounded by white bracts. It is a little less showy than *M. didyma* but more appropriate for naturalizing.

The fresh or dried leaves of bee balm are used to make refreshing, minty, citrus-scented bergamot tea.

Black-Eyed Susan

Rudbeckia

R. fulgida with coneflowers (above)
R. 'Herbstsonne' (below)

Black-eyed Susans are tough, low maintenance, long-lived perennials. Plant them wherever you want a casual look. Black-eyed Susans look great planted in drifts.

Black-eyed Susan flowers last well when cut for arrangements.

Growing

Black-eyed Susans grow well in **full sun** or **partial shade**. The soil should be of **average fertility** and **well drained**. Several *Rudbeckia* species are touted as 'claybusters' because of their tolerance for fairly heavy clay soils. Established plants tolerate drought, but regular watering is best. Divide in spring or fall, every three to five years.

Tips

Include these native plants in wildflower and natural gardens, beds and borders. Pinching the plants in June results in shorter, bushier stands.

Recommended

R. fulgida is an upright, spreading plant bearing orange-yellow flowers with brown centers. **Var.** *sullivantii* **'Goldsturm'** bears large, bright golden yellow flowers.

R. **'Herbstsonne'** is an upright, clump-forming perennial that produces bright yellow, daisy-like flowers with prominent green centers that face up to the sky. The flowers are produced from mid-summer to early fall.

R. laciniata (cutleaf coneflower) forms a large, open clump. The yellow flowers have green centers. **'Goldquelle'** has double, bright yellow flowers.

Features: bright yellow, orange or red flowers, typically with brown or green centers; attractive foliage; easy to grow **Height:** 2–6' **Spread:** 18–36" **Hardiness:** zones 3–8

Cardinal Flower

Lobelia

The brilliant red of this native flower is motivation enough for some gardeners to install a pond or bog garden, just to meet cardinal flower's requirement for moist soil.

Growing

Cardinal flowers grow well in **full sun, light shade** or **partial shade**. The soil should be **fertile, slightly acidic** and **moist**. Avoid letting the soil dry out completely, especially in a sunny location. Mulch the plants lightly in winter for protection. Deadhead to keep the plants neat and to encourage a possible second flush of blooms.

These short-lived plants tend to self-seed. The seedlings, which may not be identical to the parent plants, can be moved to new locations if desired.

Tips

These plants are best suited to streamside or pondside plantings or bog gardens. They can also be included in moist beds and borders or in any location where they will be watered regularly.

A lovely member of the bellflower family, cardinal flower contains deadly alkaloids. People have been poisoned trying to use it in herbal medicines.

L. cardinalis cultivars (above & below)

Recommended

L. cardinalis forms an upright clump of bronze green leaves and bears spikes of bright red flowers from summer to fall. Many hybrids and cultivars are available, often with flowers in shades of blue, purple, red or pink, but some are not as hardy as the species.

Features: bright red, purple, blue or pink summer flowers; bronze-green foliage
Height: 2–4' **Spread:** 12–24"
Hardiness: zones 4–9

Catmint

Nepeta

N. x faassenii (above & below)

Real workhorses in the garden bed, catmints offer season-long blooms on sturdy, trouble-free plants.

Like the other members of the mint family, catmint has square stems.

Growing

These plants prefer **full sun** or **partial shade**. Grow them in **well-drained** soil of **average fertility**; the growth tends to flop in rich soil. Plant them in spring. Divide overgrown and dense plants in spring or fall.

In June, pinch the tips to delay flowering and make the plants more compact.

Tips

Catmints form upright, spreading clumps. Plant them in herb gardens, perennial beds, rock gardens or cottage-style gardens with roses, or use them for edging borders and pathways.

Once cats discover catmint in your garden, it can be difficult to keep them out of it, because they prefer it even to *N. cataria* (catnip).

Recommended

N. '**Blue Beauty**' ('Souvenir d' André Chaudron') has gray-green foliage and large, dark purple-blue flowers.

N. **x** *faassenii* bears blue or purple flowers. Cultivars with gray-green foliage and pink, white, light purple or lavender blue flowers are available, as well as low-growing cultivars.

N. '**Six Hills Giant**' bears deep lavender blue flowers.

Features: aromatic foliage; attractive blue, purple, white or pink flowers; easy to grow
Height: 18–36" Spread: 12–24"
Hardiness: zones 3–8

Columbine
Aquilegia

*D*elicate and beautiful columbines add a touch of simple elegance to any garden. Blooming from spring through to mid-summer, these long-lasting flowers herald the passing of cool spring weather and the arrival of summer.

Growing

Columbines grow well in **light shade** or **partial shade**. They prefer soil that is **fertile, moist** and **well drained,** but they adapt to most soil conditions. Division is not required but can be used for propagation. Divided plants may take a while to recover, because columbines dislike having their roots disturbed.

Tips

Use columbines in rock gardens, formal or casual borders and naturalized or woodland gardens. Place them where other plants can fill in to hide the foliage as the columbines die back over summer.

If leaf miners are a problem, cut the foliage back once flowering is complete; new foliage will fill in.

Recommended

A. alpina (alpine columbine) grows 12–24" tall and 12" wide, bearing nodding, bright blue flowers.

A. canadensis (wild columbine, Canada columbine) is a native plant that is common in woodlands and fields. It bears yellow flowers with red spurs.

Features: spring and summer flowers in shades of red, yellow, pink, purple, blue, white or bicolored; attractive foliage
Height: 12–36" **Spread:** 12–24"
Hardiness: zones 3–8

A. vulgaris 'Nora Barlow' (above)
A. x hybrida 'McKana Hybrid' (below)

A. x hybrida (*A.* x *cultorum;* hybrid columbine) forms mounds of delicate foliage and has exceptional flowers. The many hybrids produce showy flowers in a wide range of colors.

A. vulgaris (European columbine, common columbine) has been used to develop many hybrids and cultivars with flowers in a variety of colors and forms, including double-flowered cultivars that look like frilly dahlias.

Coneflower

Echinacea

E. purpurea (above & below)

A coneflower is a visual delight, with its mauve petals offset by a spiky, orange center.

Growing

Coneflowers grow well in **full sun** or **very light shade**. They prefer an **average to rich** soil but tolerate any **well-drained** well-drained soil. Thick taproots make these plants drought resistant, but they prefer regular water. Divide every four years or so in spring or fall.

Deadhead early in the season to prolong flowering. You may wish to leave later flowerheads in place to self-seed or to provide winter interest. Pinch the plants back or thin out the stems in early summer to encourage bushy growth less prone to mildew.

Tips

Use coneflowers in meadow gardens and informal borders, either in groups or as single specimens. The dry flowerheads make an interesting fall and winter feature.

Recommended

E. purpurea is an upright plant that is covered in prickly hairs. It bears purple flowers with orangy centers. Cultivars are available, including selections with white or pink flowers. Some recent hybrids offer orange or yellow flowers.

E. tennesseensis (Tennessee coneflower) is a native wildflower that grows 12–24" tall, with a mound-forming habit. Its cupped, purple petals face upward.

Coneflowers attract wildlife to the garden, providing pollen, nectar and seeds to various hungry visitors.

Features: mid-summer to fall flowers in purple, pink, yellow, orange or white, with rusty orange centers; persistent seedheads
Height: 1–5' **Spread:** 12–24"
Hardiness: zones 3–8

Coreopsis • Tickseed

Coreopsis

*T*hese easy-to-grow plants produce flowers all summer. They make a fabulous addition to any garden.

Growing

These plants grow best in **full sun**. The soil should be of **average fertility, sandy, light** and **well drained**. Moist, cool locations with heavy soil can promote crown rot. Overly fertile soil encourages floppy growth. Deadhead to keep the plants blooming.

Tips

These versatile plants are useful in formal and informal borders and in meadow plantings and cottage-style gardens. They look best when planted in groups.

Recommended

C. auriculata 'Nana' (mouse-eared tickseed) grows about 12" tall and spreads indefinitely, albeit slowly. Well suited to rock gardens and border fronts, this low grower bears yellow-orange flowers in late spring.

C. grandiflora (bigflower coreopsis) is a clump-forming perennial that is often grown as an annual because of its prolific blooming cycle. It produces bright yellow flowers atop slender stems 12–24" tall. Cultivars offer semi-double and double flowers, differing bloom times and varied sizes.

C. lanceolata (lance coreopsis), a clump-forming perennial up to 24" tall and 18" wide, has lance-shaped leaves and solitary, yellow flowers.

C. verticillata cultivar (above)
C. grandiflora cultivar (below)

Cultivars offer dwarf forms and double flowers.

C. rosea (rose coreopsis) is a finely textured perennial with bright green foliage and yellow-centered, pink flowers from summer to fall. '**Sweet Dreams**' has fine, needle-like foliage and large, white flowers with dark pinkish-purple rings surrounding a yellow center.

C. verticillata (thread-leaf coreopsis) is a mound-forming plant 24–32" tall and 18" wide with attractive finely divided foliage and bright yellow flowers. Cultivars offer pale yellow blooms and reduced height.

Features: yellow, orange, white or pink summer flowers; attractive foliage
Height: 12–32" **Spread:** 12" to indefinite
Hardiness: zones 3–9

Daylily
Hemerocallis

'Dewey Roquemore' (above), 'Bonanza' (below)

Growing

Daylilies bloom best in **full sun** but also grow in full shade. The soil should be **fertile, moist** and **well drained,** although these plants adapt to most conditions and are hard to kill once established. Divide every two or three years to keep the plants vigorous and blooming profusely. They can, however, be left indefinitely without dividing. Deadhead to prolong the blooming period. Cut foliage back to the ground to produce lush new growth.

Be careful when deadheading purple-flowered daylilies, because the sap can stain fingers and clothes.

Tips

Plant daylilies alone or group them in borders, on banks and in ditches to control erosion. They can be naturalized in woodland or meadow gardens. Small varieties are also nice in planters.

The adaptability and durability of daylilies—combined with their variety in color, blooming period, size and texture—explain their popularity.

Recommended

Daylily species, cultivars and hybrids come in an almost infinite number of forms, sizes and colors. Several repeat-blooming varieties, which bloom on and off during the growing season, are now on the market. Visit your local garden center or daylily grower to find out what's available and most suitable for your garden.

Features: spring and summer flowers in every color except blue or pure white; grass-like foliage **Height:** 1–4' **Spread:** 1–4' **Hardiness:** zones 2–8

Gaura

Gaura

The pink and white flowers floating high above gaura's tall, slender stems resemble butterflies whirling in the sunlight.

Growing

Gaura prefers **full sun** but tolerates partial shade. The soil should be **fertile, moist** and **well drained**. A deep taproot helps established plants tolerate drought but makes division difficult.

Deadhead gaura to keep it flowering right up until the end of the season, prevent excessive self-seeding and keep the plant tidy.

Tips

Gaura makes a good addition for borders. Its color and appearance have a softening effect on brighter colors. Although it bears only a few flowers at a time, it blooms for the entire summer. It is most effective when used en masse or with large, bold plants in the background as a backdrop.

Recommended

G. **lindheimeri** (white gaura) is a clump-forming plant. It bears clusters of star-shaped, white flowers from pink buds. The flowers fade back to pink with age. **'Siskiyou Pink'** is a shorter variety, with bright pink flowers and foliage that is marked with reddish purple. **'Whirling Butterflies'** grows up to 36" tall and tends to have more flowers in bloom at a time.

G. lindheimeri (above & below)

Heat-tolerant and sun-loving gaura, with its wiry stems of delicate blooms, provides a textural contrast for the thick, rounded leaves of succulents and broad-leaved plants.

Features: delicate pink and white flowers; scarlet stems in winter; decorative habit
Height: 2–4' **Spread:** 24–36"
Hardiness: zones 6–9

Goldenrod

Solidago

'Crown of Rays' (above & below)

The cultivated varieties of golden-rod tame the unruly appearance of the native species but keep the profusion of bloom.

Ragweed (Ambrosia species), not goldenrod, is the source of hay-fever pollen.

Growing

Goldenrod prefers **full sun** but tolerates partial shade. The soil should be of **poor to average fertility, light** and **well drained**. Too fertile a soil results in lush growth, few flowers and invasive behavior.

Divide goldenrod every three to five years in spring or fall to keep it vigorous and to control growth.

Tips

Goldenrod is great for providing late-season color. It looks at home in a large border or a cottage-style or wildflower garden. Don't plant it near less vigorous plants, because goldenrod can quickly overwhelm them. Goldenrod is a great plant for xeriscaping.

Recommended

Solidago **hybrids** form a clump of strong stems with narrow leaves. They grow about 2–4' tall and spread about 18–24". Plume-like clusters of yellow flowers are produced from mid-summer to fall. **'Crown of Rays'** holds its flower clusters in horizontal spikes and flowers from mid-summer to fall. **'Fireworks'** has strong, sturdy stems and golden yellow flower spikes that dart horizontally throughout the clump of foliage. **'Golden Shower'** bears flowers in horizontal or drooping plumes.

Features: yellow flowers from mid-summer through fall; attractive habit **Height:** 2–4' **Spread:** 18–30" **Hardiness:** zones 3–8

Heliopsis
Heliopsis

*O*f flowers send messages, heliopsis sings out, 'It's fun in the sun!' Combine this bright character with butterfly weed, asters and ornamental grasses for a look that is unforgettable.

Growing

Heliopsis prefers **full sun** but tolerates partial shade. The soil should be **average to fertile, humus rich, moist** and **well drained**. Most soil conditions are tolerated, including poor, dry soils. Divide every two or so years.

Deadhead to prolong the blooming period. Cut the plants back once flowering is complete.

Tips

Use heliopsis at the back or in the middle of mixed or herbaceous borders. This easy-to-grow plant is popular with novice gardeners.

Recommended

H. helianthoides forms an upright clump of stems and foliage and bears daisy-like, yellow or orange flowers. A variety of cultivars offer unique characteristics. **'Summer Sun'** ('Sommersonne') bears single or semidouble flowers in bright golden yellow. It grows about 36" tall.

H. helianthoides (above & below)

The stiff stems of heliopsis are an advantage in fresh-flower arrangements.

Features: bright yellow or orange flowers
Height: 3–5' **Spread:** 18–36"
Hardiness: zones 2–9

Hosta

Hosta

H. sieboldiana 'Elegans' (above)
Variegated cultivar (below)

Breeders are always looking for new variations in hosta foliage. Swirls, stripes, puckers and ribs enhance the various sizes, shapes and colors of the leaves.

Growing

Most hostas prefer **light or partial shade** but also grow in full shade, although some sun-loving varieties are now available. The ideal soil is **fertile, moist** and **well drained,** but most soils are tolerated. Morning sun is preferable to afternoon sun in partial shade situations. Hostas are fairly drought tolerant, especially with a mulch to help them retain moisture.

Division is not required but can be done every few years in spring or summer to propagate new plants.

Tips

Hostas make wonderful woodland plants and look very attractive when combined with ferns and other fine-textured plants. They are also good in a mixed border, particularly when used to hide the ugly leggy lower stems and branches of some shrubs. The dense growth and thick, shade-providing leaves allow hostas to suppress weeds. Hostas are very effective visually when used en masse or in odd-numbered groups.

Recommended

Hosta cultivars number in the hundreds, thanks to crossbreeding and hybridizing. Visit your local garden center or get a mail-order catalog to find out what's available.

Also called: plantain lily **Features:** decorative foliage; summer and fall flowers in white or purple **Height:** 4–36" **Spread:** 6"–6' **Hardiness:** zones 3–8

Lamb's Ears

Stachys

Named for its soft, fuzzy leaves, lamb's ears has silvery foliage that is a beautiful contrast to any bold-colored plants that tower above it.

Growing

Lamb's ears grows best in **full sun**. The soil should be of **poor** or **average fertility** and **well drained**. The leaves can rot in humid weather if the soil is poorly drained. Remove spent flower spikes to keep the plants looking neat.

Tips

Lamb's ears makes a great groundcover in a new garden where the soil has not yet been amended. When used to edge borders and pathways, it provides a soft, silvery backdrop for more vibrant colors next to it. For a silvery accent, plant a small group of lamb's ears in a border.

Recommended

S. *byzantina* forms a mat of thick, woolly rosettes of leaves. Pinkish purple flowers bloom in early summer. The species can be quite invasive, so choosing a cultivar may be wise. The many cultivars offer a variety of foliage colors, sizes and flowers. **'Helene von Stein'** ('Big Ears'), is a clump-forming perennial that produces fuzzy leaves twice as large as those of other species or cultivars.

S. byzantina (above & below)

Many plants in the mint family contain antibacterial and antifungal compounds. Lamb's ears not only feels soft, but it may actually encourage healing.

Also called: lamb's tails, lamb's tongues
Features: soft and fuzzy, silver foliage; pink or purple flowers **Height:** 6–18"
Spread: 18–24" **Hardiness:** zones 3–8

Lenten Rose • Hellebore

Helleborus

H. foetidus (above & below)

These beautiful spring-blooming groundcovers are among the earliest harbingers of spring, providing a welcome hint of what's to come long before most other plants have even started to sprout.

Growing

These plants prefer **light, dappled shade** and a **sheltered location** but tolerate some direct sun in evenly moist soil. The soil should be **fertile, humus rich, neutral to alkaline, moist** and **well drained**. Mulch the plants in winter if they are in an exposed location.

Tips

Use these plants in a sheltered border or rock garden, or naturalize them in a woodland garden.

Many hellebores have evergreen leaves and may flower as early as January.

Recommended

H. foetidus (bear's-foot hellebore) grows 30" tall and wide. It bears dark green leaves and clusters of light green flowers with purplish red edges. Cultivars offer larger sizes and varied flower colors.

H. x hybridus plants grow about 18" tall, with an equal spread. They may be deciduous or evergreen, and they bloom in a wide range of colors. Cultivars offer deeper colored, double, spotted and picotee flowers.

H. orientalis (lenten rose) is a clump-forming, evergreen perennial. It grows 12–24" tall, with an equal spread. It bears white or greenish flowers that turn pink as they mature in mid- or late spring.

Features: mid-winter to mid-spring flowers in white, green, pink, purple, yellow or picotee **Height:** 12–30" **Spread:** 12–30" **Hardiness:** zones 5–9

Obedient Plant

Physostegia

Hummingbirds love to sip from the tiny, snapdragon-like flowers, so place your obedient plant where you can watch the show.

Growing

Obedient plant prefers **full sun** but tolerates partial or light shade. The soil should be **moist** and of **average to high fertility**. In fertile soil, this plant is more vigorous and may need staking. To curtail invasiveness, divide every two years or so in early to mid-spring, once the soil can be worked.

Tips

Use obedient plant in borders, cottage-style gardens and informal borders, and for naturalizing. The flowers can be cut for use in fresh arrangements.

Recommended

P. virginiana has a spreading root system from which upright stems sprout. The species bears sharply toothed foliage and deep purple, bright purple-pink or sometimes white flower spikes. The species can reach 4' in height. Cultivars are available in smaller, compact forms with pink, white or purple flowers. **'Pink Bouquet'** bears bright pink flowers. **'Variegata'** produces variegated foliage with cream-margined leaves and bright pink flowers.

P. virginiana (above & below)

The individual flowers of obedient plant can be bent around on the stems and will stay put where you leave them. This unusual trait is responsible for the plant's common name.

Features: mid-summer to fall flowers in purple, pink or white; attractive habit
Height: 1–4' **Spread:** 12–24"
Hardiness: zones 2–9

Peony

Paeonia

P. lactiflora cultivars (above & below)

From the simple, single flowers to the extravagant doubles, it's easy to become mesmerized by these voluptuous plants. Once the fleeting, but magnificent, flower display is done, the foliage remains stellar throughout the growing season.

Growing

Peonies prefer **full sun** but tolerate some shade. They like **fertile, humus-rich, moist, well-drained** soil to which a lot of **compost** has been added. The site should be well prepared before planting. Mulch is unnecessary, because peonies like winter's cold. Too much fertilizer, particularly nitrogen, causes floppy growth and retards blooming. Deadhead to keep the plants looking tidy.

Place wire peony rings or grids around the plants in late winter to support the heavy flowers. The foliage will grow up and through the wires, hiding the supports.

Tips

These wonderful plants look great in a border combined with other early bloomers. The foliage begins to emerge in late winter. Avoid planting peonies under trees, where they will have to compete for moisture and nutrients.

Planting depth determines whether a peony will flower. Tubers planted too deep will not flower. The buds or eyes on the tuber should be barely below the soil surface.

Recommended

Hundreds of peony selections are available. The single or double flowers come in a wide range of colors and may be fragrant. Choose heat-tolerant varieties that won't 'melt down' in the heat of summer. Visit your local garden center to see what is available.

Peonies are guaranteed to attract ants once flowering begins. The ants do not cause any damage but just feed on the sugary nectar of the flowers.

Features: white, cream white, yellow, pink, red or purple spring flowers; attractive foliage
Height: 24–32" **Spread:** 24–32"
Hardiness: zones 2–8

Perennial Salvia

Salvia

Choosing from the most numerous genus of the mint family can be overwhelming, but perennial salvias are a staple of the South. The *Salvia* genus touches upon every category of plants, and perennials are no exception.

Growing

Salvia plants prefer **full sun** but tolerate light shade. The soil should be **moist, very well drained** and of **average to rich fertility,** with a lot of **organic matter**. Apply mulch after the first hard frost in fall.

Tips

Most salvia selections are used as border fillers, but salvias are also useful in cutting gardens, cottage-style gardens and for naturalizing.

Recommended

S. guaranitica (anise sage, Brazilian sage) is the one truly hardy perennial salvia for Tennessee. This upright plant grows 4–5' tall and wide, with a branching habit. Cobalt blue flowers are displayed from spring to fall. **'Argentine Skies'** has light blue flowers. **'Black and Blue'** is a shorter selection with deep blue blossoms and dark bluish purple calyxes.

Salvias make great cut flowers and attract butterflies and hummingbirds.

S. leucantha (above), *S. guaranitica* (below)

Tender perennial salvias are great for a season or two, but none are reliable repeat performers. A vast array of selections are available. *S. involucrata* (rosebud sage) bears rose-pink flowers. *S. leucantha* (Mexican bush sage) produces long, velvety purple flower spikes. *S. madrensis* (forsythia sage) has yellow flower spikes. Consult your local garden center for recommendations based on your area.

Features: blue, yellow, pink or purple flower spikes; attractive habit **Height:** 4–5'
Spread: 3–5' **Hardiness:** zones 8–10

Phlox

Phlox

P. subulata (above), *P. paniculata* (below)

Phloxes come in many shapes and sizes, with flowering periods falling anywhere between early spring and mid-fall.

Growing

Phloxes prefer **full sun** and **fertile, humus-rich, moist, well-drained** soil. Divide them in fall or spring.

Tips

Low-growing species are useful in rock gardens or at the front of borders. Taller phloxes may be used in the middle of borders and are particularly effective if planted in groups.

Recommended

P. maculata (Carolina phlox, thick-leaf phlox, early phlox, garden phlox, wild sweet William) forms an upright clump of hairy stems and narrow leaves that are sometimes spotted with red. Pink, purple or white flowers are borne in conical clusters.

P. paniculata (garden phlox, summer phlox) is an upright plant. The many cultivars vary in size and flower color.

P. subulata (moss phlox) is a creeping groundcover that flowers in shades of white, pink or purple.

The name Phlox *is from the Greek word for 'flame,' referring to the colorful flowers of many species.*

Features: spring, summer or fall flowers in shades of white, blue, purple, pink, red or bicolored, often with a colored or contrasting central eye **Height:** 4"–5' **Spread:** 12–24" **Hardiness:** zones 4–8

Pinks

Dianthus

From tiny and delicate to large and robust, this genus contains a wide variety of plants, many with spice-scented flowers.

Growing

Pinks prefer **full sun** but tolerate some light shade. A **neutral to alkaline, well-drained** soil is required. Drainage is the most important factor in the successful cultivation of pinks—they hate to stand in water. Rocky outcroppings are the native habitat of many species.

Tips

Pinks make excellent plants for rock gardens and rock walls and for edging flower borders and walkways. They can also be used in cutting gardens and even as groundcovers. To prolong blooming, deadhead as the flowers fade, but leave a few flowers in place to go to seed.

Recommended

D.* x *allwoodii (Allwood pinks) hybrids form compact mounds and bear flowers in a wide range of colors. Many cultivars are available.

D. deltoides (maiden pink) forms a mat of foliage and bears flowers in shades of red.

Pinks self-seed quite easily. The seedlings may differ from the parent plants, often with new and interesting results.

D. gratianopolitanus 'Bath's Pink' (above)
D. plumarius (below)

D. gratianopolitanus (cheddar pink) is long-lived and forms a very dense mat of evergreen, silver gray foliage with sweet-scented flowers, mostly in shades of pink.

D. plumarius (cottage pink) is noteworthy for its role in the development of many popular cultivars known collectively as garden pinks. The flowers can be single, semi-double or fully double and are available in many colors.

Features: sometimes-fragrant spring or summer flowers in shades of pink, red, white or purple; attractive foliage **Height:** 2–18" **Spread:** 6–24" **Hardiness:** zones 3–9

Russian Sage
Perovskia

P. atriplicifolia (above), *P. atriplicifolia* 'Filigran' (below)

Russian sage offers four-season interest: soft, gray-green leaves on light gray stems in spring; fuzzy, violet blue flowers in summer; and silvery white stems from fall until late winter.

Growing

Russian sage prefers **full sun**. The soil should be **poor to moderately fertile** and **well drained**. Too much water and nitrogen cause this plant's growth to flop, so do not plant it next to heavy feeders. Because Russian sage is a subshrub that originates from a single stem, it cannot be divided.

To encourage vigorous, bushy growth, cut the plant back hard to about 6–12" in spring, when new growth appears low on the branches, or in fall.

Tips

The silvery foliage and blue flowers of Russian sage soften the appearance of daylilies and work well with other plants in the back of a mixed border. Russian sage can also create a soft screen in a natural garden or on a dry bank.

Recommended

P. atriplicifolia is a loose, upright plant with silvery white, finely divided foliage. The small, lavender blue flowers are loosely held on branched, silvery stems. Cultivars are available.

Russian sage blossoms make a lovely addition to fresh bouquets and dried-flower arrangements.

Features: lavender blue flowers in mid-summer to fall; attractive habit; fragrant, gray-green foliage **Height:** 3–4' **Spread:** 3–4' **Hardiness:** zones 4–9

Sedum

Sedum

Sedum is a large and diverse genus of over 300 different species, including many that do very well in the South.

Growing

Sedums prefer **full sun** but tolerate partial shade. The soil should be of **average fertility** and **very well drained**. Divide in spring when necessary.

Tips

Low-growing sedum selections make wonderful groundcovers and additions to rock gardens, rock walls, beds and borders. Taller sedums are excellent for a late-season display in a bed or border.

Recommended

Low-growing, wide-spreading selections (2–6" tall and 24" wide) include **S. acre** (gold moss stonecrop), which bears small, yellow-green flowers; **S. reflexum** (stone orpine), which has needle-like, blue-green foliage (Zones 6–9); and **S. spurium** (two-row stonecrop), which has deep pink or white flowers. Many cultivars with colorful foliage are available.

Early-summer pruning of upright species and hybrids encourages compact, bushy growth but can delay flowering.

S. *spurium* 'Dragon's Blood' (above)
S. 'Autumn Joy' (below)

Tall selections (18–24" tall and wide) include **S. 'Autumn Joy'**, with flowers that open pink or red and later fade to deep bronze (Zones 3–10); and **S. spectabile** (showy stonecrop), with blooms in white and various shades of pink. (Zones 3–8).

Also called: stonecrop **Features:** yellow, yellow-green, white, red and pink summer to fall flowers; decorative, fleshy foliage
Height: 2–24 **Spread:** 10–24" or more
Hardiness: zones 3–8

Spiked Speedwell
Veronica

V. spicata 'Red Fox' (above & below)

Spiked speedwells punctuate the front or middle of a garden bed with spikes of white, pink or violet flowers.

Growing

Spiked speedwells prefer **full sun** but tolerate partial shade. The soil should be of **average fertility, moist** and **well drained**. Established plants tolerate short periods of drought. Lack of sun and excessive moisture and nitrogen may contribute to the sloppy habits of some speedwells. To ensure strong, vigorous growth and to reduce flopping, divide the plants every two or three years in spring.

When the flowers begin to fade, remove the entire spike where it joins the plant to encourage rapid re-blooming.

Tips

Spiked speedwells work well at the front of a perennial border, as groundcovers or contained in rock gardens. They are also quite striking when planted in masses in a bed or border.

Recommended

V. spicata is a low, mounding plant with stems that flop over when they get too tall. It bears spikes of blue flowers. Many cultivars with different flower colors are available.

V. **'Sunny Border Blue'** is a clump-forming perennial 18–20" tall and 12" wide, with toothed, glossy leaves. It flowers nonstop throughout the growing season, bearing dark violet blue flowers.

Spiked speedwells combine well with lilies, yarrow, shrub roses and daisy-flowered perennials.

Features: white, pink, purple or blue summer flowers; varied habits **Height:** 6–24"
Spread: 12–24" **Hardiness:** zones 3–8

American Hop Hornbeam
Ostrya

O. virginiana (left & right)

American hop hornbeam is a lovely, sturdy and stately tree deserving of wider use. It's slow to grow but well worth the wait.

Growing
This tree prefers **full sun;** partial shade is acceptable but results in slower growth. For best growth, the soil should be **slightly acidic** and **well drained**.

Tips
American hop hornbeam's dense canopy and preference for acidic soils make it ideal for woodland settings. It is often planted as an understory tree as well. This ideal urban tree also performs well as a lone specimen in rural settings. It can provide a lot of shade in sunny locations.

Recommended
O. virginiana (ironwood) is a conical tree with a dense growth habit and roughly textured, toothed foliage. It bears pendulous, yellow male catkins and white female fruit that closely resembles that of hops, hence the common name.

The very hard and dense wood of American hop hornbeam was once used for items subject to prolonged friction, including sleigh runners, wheel rims and airplane propellers.

Features: attractive and unusual flowers and fruit; attractive habit **Habit:** dense, conical, deciduous tree **Height:** 40–50' **Spread:** 40' **Hardiness:** zones 5–9

Arborvitae
Thuja

T. occidentalis 'Little Gem' (above)
T. occidentalis (below)

Arborvitae are rot resistant, durable and long-lived, earning quiet admiration from gardeners everywhere.

Growing
Arborvitae prefer **full sun** but tolerate light or partial shade. The soil should be of **average fertility, moist** and **well drained**. These plants enjoy humidity and are often found near marshy areas in the wild. Arborvitae like some shelter from wind, especially in winter, when the foliage can easily dry out and assume a drab brown appearance.

Tips
The large varieties of arborvitae make excellent specimen trees; smaller cultivars can be used in foundation plantings and shrub borders and as formal or informal hedges.

Recommended
T. occidentalis (eastern arborvitae, eastern white cedar) is a narrow, pyramidal tree with scale-like, evergreen needles. Cultivars include shrubby, dwarf varieties, varieties with yellow foliage and small, upright varieties. (Zones 2–7; some cultivars may be less cold hardy)

T. orientalis (oriental aborvitae) grows 25' tall and 15' wide. The species is rarely available, but cultivars and hybrids offer varied coloration and forms and overall diversity. **'Degroot's Spire'** is a slow-growing, upright variety with deep green foliage and a mature size of 6' tall and 24" wide. **'Golden Globe'** develops a rounded, dwarf form with golden yellow foliage.

T. plicata (American arborvitae, western arborvitae, western red cedar) is a deer-resistant, quick-growing, narrowly pyramidal, evergreen tree that maintains good foliage color all winter. Cultivars include several dwarf varieties and a variegated, yellow-and-green selection. **'Green Giant'** can grow 3–5' annually, eventually reaching 30–50' in height and 10–20' in spread. (Zones 5–9)

Features: attractive foliage, bark and habit
Habit: small to large, evergreen shrub or tree
Height: 2–50' **Spread:** 2–20'
Hardiness: zones 2–9

Barberry
Berberis

As dependable, easy-to-grow shrubs with many variations in plant size, foliage color and fruit, barberries are real workhorses.

Growing

Barberries develop the best fall color and most fruit when grown in **full sun,** but they tolerate partial shade. Any **well-drained** soil is suitable. Barberries tolerate drought and urban conditions but suffer in poorly drained, wet soil.

Tips

Large barberries make great hedges. Barberries can also be included in shrub and mixed borders. Small cultivars can be grown in rock gardens, in raised beds and along rock walls.

Recommended

B. darwinii (Darwin's barberry) is an evergreen shrub that bears small, yellow flowers in spring and sometimes again in fall. The small berries are dark blue. This species is not as spiny as the others.

B. x mentorensis (Mentor barberry) is a large, generally deciduous shrub with even, dense growth, impassable spines, yellow spring flowers and attractive fall color.

Extracts from the rhizomes of Berberis *have been used to treat rheumatic fever and other inflammatory disorders as well as the common cold.*

B. thunbergii 'Crimson Pygmy' (above)
B. thunbergii 'Atropurpurea' (below)

B. thunbergii (Japanese barberry) is a broad, rounded, dense shrub with bright green foliage and orange, red or purple fall color. It bears yellow spring flowers and glossy, red fruit. Many cultivars have foliage that may be variegated or shades of purple or yellow.

Features: attractive foliage; yellow flowers; fruit; formidable spines **Habit:** prickly deciduous shrub **Height:** 1–6' **Spread:** 18"–6' **Hardiness:** zones 4–8

Black Gum

Nyssa

N. sylvatica (above), N. sylvatica cultivar (below)

Black gum fruit attracts birds but is too sour for human tastes.

Black gum shines with bright green foliage in summer, giving way to a lovely fall show in shades of yellow, orange, scarlet and purple.

Growing

Black gum grows well in **full sun** or **partial shade**. The soil should be **average to fertile, neutral to acidic** and **well drained**. Provide a location with shelter from strong winds. Plant this tree when young and don't attempt to move it again. It can take a while to get established and dislikes having its roots disturbed.

Tips

Black gum is a beautiful specimen tree. It can be used as a street tree, but not in polluted situations. Singly or in groups, it is attractive and small enough for a medium-sized property.

Recommended

N. sylvatica (sour gum, black tupelo) is a small to medium-sized, pyramidal to rounded tree. It generally grows 30–50' tall but can reach 100' over time. It spreads about 20–30'. Cultivars offer special characteristics. **'Autumn Cascade'** is a weeping selection. **'Forum,'** features a conical form.

Features: attractive habit; decorative foliage; fall color **Habit:** pyramidal to rounded, deciduous tree **Height:** 10–50' or more **Spread:** 6–30' **Hardiness:** zones 4–9

Boxwood

Buxus

Boxwood's dense growth and small leaves form an even, green surface, which, along with its slow rate of growth, make this plant among the most popular for creating low hedges and topiaries.

Growing

Boxwoods prefer **partial shade** but adapt to full sun if kept well watered. The soil should be **fertile** and **well drained**. Established plants tolerate drought. Boxwood roots grow very close to the surface and are easily damaged if the surrounding soil is disturbed. They benefit from a good, rich mulch.

Tips

Boxwoods make excellent background plants in a mixed border, providing a uniformly dark green backdrop for colorful flowers. Dwarf cultivars can be trimmed into small hedges for edging garden beds or walkways. An interesting topiary piece can create a formal or whimsical focal point in any garden. Large selections are often used for dense, evergreen hedges.

Recommended

B. microphylla **var.** *koreana* (Korean boxwood) grows about 4' tall, with an equal spread. The bright green foliage may turn bronze, brown or yellow in winter. It is hardy to zone 4. Cultivars are available.

B. sempervirens (common boxwood), left unpruned, can grow up to 20' tall, with an equal spread. **'Suffruticosa'** (edging boxwood) is a compact, slow growing cultivar that's often used as hedging. **'Wintergreen'** retains its dark green coloration throughout winter. Other cultivars are also available in varied sizes and forms.

Some of the best boxwood selections are cultivars developed from crosses between the two above species. They possess a high level of pest resistance and vigor, with attractive winter color. *B.* CHICAGOLAND GREEN, *B.* **'Green Mountain'** and *B.* **'Green Velvet'** are selections well suited for Tennessee.

Features: attractive foliage **Habit:** dense, rounded, evergreen shrub **Height:** 2–20' **Spread:** 2–20' **Hardiness:** zones 4–8

Boxwood foliage contains toxic compounds that, when ingested, can cause severe digestive upset.

Burning Bush • Euonymus
Euonymus

E. alatus 'Cole's Select' (above), *E. elatus* (below)

Few plants can match the stunning fall color of burning bush, a popular kind of *Euonymous*.

Growing

Burning bush prefers **full sun** and tolerates light or partial shade. Soil of **average to rich fertility** is preferable, but any **moist, well-drained** soil will do.

Tips

Burning bush can be grown in a shrub or mixed border, as a specimen, in a naturalistic garden or as a hedge. Dwarf cultivars can be used to create informal hedges.

Recommended

E. alatus (burning bush, winged euonymus) is an attractive, open, mounding, deciduous shrub with corky ridges on the stems and branches. The fall foliage is a vivid red. Cultivars are available, including a dwarf selection.

The name Euonymus *means 'of good name,' an ironic translation given that all parts of these plants are* **poisonous** *and violently purgative.*

Features: fall color; corky stems; attractive habit **Habit:** vase-shaped, deciduous shrub **Height:** 2–10' **Spread:** 2–6' **Hardiness:** zones 3–8

Butterfly Bush

Buddleia (Buddleja)

Butterfly bushes are among the best shrubs for attracting butterflies and bees to a garden. Don't spray your bush for pests—doing so would also harm the beautiful and beneficial insects.

Growing

Butterfly bushes prefer to grow in **full sun;** shade results in fewer flowers. The soil should be **average to fertile** and **well drained**. Established shrubs tolerate drought.

Tips

Its graceful, arching branches make butterfly bush an excellent specimen plant and a beautiful addition to shrub or mixed borders.

To control this very fast-growing shrub, cut it back heavily in spring, leaving just 12" stumps, and it will still bloom the same summer.

Deadhead spent blooms to promote heavy flowering all season.

Recommended

B. alternifolia (alternate-leaved butterfly bush) can be trained to form a small tree. In late spring or early summer, clusters of light purple flowers form on the ends of the branches.

B. davidii (above & below)

B. davidii (orange eye butterfly bush, summer lilac) bears flowers in bright and pastel shades of purple, white, pink or blue from mid-summer to fall. Many cultivars are available. (Zones 5–8)

Butterfly bushes can self-seed. You may find tiny bushes popping up in unlikely places around the garden.

Features: attractive flowers, habit and foliage
Habit: deciduous, large shrub or small tree with arching branches **Height:** 4–20'
Spread: 4–20' **Hardiness:** zones 4–8

Carolina Silverbell

Halesia

H. tetraptera (above & below)

into single-stemmed trees unless you want them to grow into large shrub forms. Prune only after flowering.

Tips

Commonly considered to be an understory tree, Carolina silverbell grows quite happily under the canopy of larger trees. It is ideal for that moist location where few other trees will grow. This spring bloomer is the perfect specimen for the front yard, without overpowering the front of a house. Dappled sunlight will travel through the branches, giving light shade to plants below.

N ative to the South, this lovely specimen tree is a must-have for gardeners who desire a prolific spring bloomer with much to offer.

Growing

Carolina silverbell prefers **partial shade** but tolerates full sun. The soil should be **rich, moist** and **very well drained,** and amended with **organic matter**. **Mulching** is imperative to prevent the soil from drying out. Prune as necessary but train any multi-stemmed specimens

Recommended

H. tetraptera is a small to medium-sized tree that displays an open form and produces pendent, bell-shaped, white flowers along each branch in early spring. Yellowish green fruit follows after the flowers, adding further interest in fall. Cultivars are available, including a pink-flowering selection called **'Rosea.'**

Carolina silverbell is especially striking when planted in front of a background of evergreens.

Features: pendent, white flowers; attractive form; attractive fruit **Habit:** open, low-branched, rounded, small to medium tree **Height:** 30–40' **Spread:** 20–35' **Hardiness:** zones 5–8

Crape Myrtle
Lagerstroemia

Most Southern gardeners couldn't imagine the Southern landscape without crape myrtles. These plants offer a unique element to just about any setting and require little care, with stunning results.

Growing

Crape myrtles prefer **full sun,** which helps prevent mildew, but tolerate light shade. They like **well-drained, neutral to slightly acidic soil**. In alkaline or salty soil, they may experience burning of the leaf margins or chlorosis. Hot winds may also scorch the leaf margins.

Young plants require regular water. Established plants tolerate drought but like an occasional deep watering. Do not water from overhead. Fertilize with organic fertilizer in late winter, before the new growth emerges. Prune suckers away as they appear. Remove any newly emerging seedlings. A long, cool fall yields the best leaf color.

Tips

Crape myrtles make excellent specimens or can be mass planted. *L. indica* is suitable as a street tree and in lawns. Row-planted crape myrtles can be used for hedging, screening and shrub borders.

Take care when selecting plants for underplanting around crape myrtles—the roots are quite competitive.

Features: flower clusters in shades of white, pink, red, purple or coral; exfoliating bark; fall color **Height:** 8–30' **Spread:** 6–16' **Hardiness:** zones 7–9

L. indica

Recommended

L. fauriei (Japanese crape myrtle) is a medium-sized, erect tree with outward-arching branches. It bears lush green leaves, attractive bark, and clusters of small, white flowers. Many cultivars exist. **'Fantasy'** produces showier bark and a vase-like form.

L. indica is a small, multi-stemmed tree or large shrub with showy clusters of ruffled, crepe-like flowers in white and shades of red, pink and purple all summer. The foliage begins as bronze-tinged light green, aging to dark glossy green in summer and turning yellow, orange or red in fall. The gray-brown bark exfoliates, revealing pinkish bark beneath. Standard and dwarf varieties are available. **'Carolina Beauty'** bears dark red flower clusters and orange fall foliage. **'Natchez,'** a vigorous grower with white flowers, is rarely affected by powdery mildew.

Cryptomeria
Cryptomeria

C. japonica 'Black Dragon' (above)
C. japonica (below)

What would a Southern garden be without the graceful addition of a tall, evergreen specimen such as cryptomeria? With so much to offer year-round, cryptomeria is a must-have tree for gardens throughout the state.

An endless supply of cryptomeria selections is available for almost every gardening application, including foundation planting, large tree specimens and mixed beds and borders.

Growing

Cryptomeria prefers **full sun** or **light shade**. The soil should be **fertile, well drained, rich** and **deep**. Plant cryptomeria higher in the ground in heavily clay-based soil and lower in soil that has been deeply amended. Mulch well to prevent drying out during periods of drought.

Tips

Tall conifers such as cryptomeria are often used as specimens in residential landscapes and gardens. They're also planted for screening purposes.

Recommended

C. japonica is a vigorously growing tree with a slightly columnar habit, pendulous branches and attractive exfoliating, thin, reddish brown bark. The needle-like, bright green to bluish green leaves turn brown-purple toward fall. **'Benjamin Franklin'** develops into a tall tree with foliage that remains green year-round. It is highly tolerant of wind and salt. **'Black Dragon'** bears light green foliage that darkens to almost black in fall. It grows more slowly, reaching only 5' tall and 7' wide over a 10-year period. **'Elegans'** is a grayish green cultivar that turns coppery red in winter. It can grow quite tall and wide. **'Pygmaea'** is a dwarf selection that grows only 12–24" tall and wide. **'Yoshino'** is similar to the species, but smaller.

Features: year-round foliage; winter color; attractive habit **Habit:** conical or columnar, coniferous tree or shrub of variable size
Height: 1–100' **Spread:** 1–30'
Hardiness: zones 6–8

Dogwood
Cornus

Whether your garden is wet, dry, sunny or shaded, there is a dogwood for almost every condition. Stem color, leaf variegation, fall color, growth habit, soil adaptability and hardiness are some of the dogwood's positive attributes.

Growing

Dogwoods grow almost equally well in **full sun, light shade** or **partial shade,** with a slight preference for light shade. The soil should be of **average to high fertility, high in organic matter, neutral or slightly acidic** and **well drained.**

Tips

Shrub dogwoods can be included in a shrub or mixed border. They look best in groups rather than as single specimens. The tree species make wonderful specimen plants and are small enough to include in most gardens. Use them along the edge of a woodland, in a shrub or mixed border, alongside a house, or near a pond, water feature or patio.

Recommended

C. florida (flowering dogwood) is a conical tree or shrub with slightly twisted or curled foliage that turns a brilliant red and purple in fall. The yellow-tipped, green spring flowers are surrounded by large, white to pink bracts; bright red fruit often follows. The many cultivars offer vivid bract colors and variegated leaves.

C. *florida* cultivar (above)
C. *kousa* var. *chinensis* (below)

'**Cherokee Brave**' bears white-marked, red bracts. '**Cherokee Princess**' produces white bracts. '**Rubra**' has pink or rose pink bracts.

C. kousa (Kousa dogwood) has interesting bark and bears white-bracted flowers and bright red fruit. The foliage turns red and purple in fall. **Var.** *chinensis* (Chinese dogwood) grows more vigorously and has larger flowers. '**Satomi**' has soft pink bracts.

Features: white-, pink- or ruby-bracted flowers in late spring and early summer; fall color; fruit; interesting stems and bark
Habit: deciduous, large shrub or small tree
Height: 5–30' **Spread:** 5–30'
Hardiness: zones 5–9

False Cypress
Chamaecyparis

C. pisifera 'Mops' (above)

Conifer shoppers are blessed with a marvelous selection of false cypresses that offer color, size, shape and growth habits not available in most other evergreens.

Growing

False cypresses prefer **full sun or partial shade**. The soil should be **fertile, moist, neutral to acidic** and **well drained**. Alkaline soils are tolerated. In shaded areas, growth may be sparse or thin.

Tips

Tree varieties are used as specimen plants and for hedging. The dwarf and slow-growing cultivars are used in borders, rock gardens and as bonsai. False cypress shrubs can be grown near the house or as evergreen specimens in large containers.

Recommended

Several species and many cultivars are available. The scaly foliage, in dark green, bright green or yellow, can be in a drooping or strand-like form or in fan-like or feathery sprays. Varied habits include mounding to rounded, tall and pyramidal, and narrow with pendulous branches.

C. obtusa (Hinoki cypress) is a broad, conical tree up to 70' tall, with dark green foliage. '**Nana Gracilis**' is a smaller, pyramidal cultivar that grows only 10' tall.

C. pisifera (Sawara cypress) grows up to 70' tall and 15' wide, with a more open habit and flattened sprays of bright green foliage. '**Filifera**' is a cultivar with slender branches and dark green foliage. '**Filifera Aurea**' grows up to 40' tall and bears golden yellow leaves. Check with your local garden center or nursery to see what is available.

Features: attractive foliage and habit; cones **Habit:** narrow, pyramidal, evergreen tree or shrub **Height:** 2–70' **Spread:** 2–20 **Hardiness:** zones 4–8

Flowering Crabapple
Crabapple

Malus

Loads of spring flowers, a brilliant display of colorful fall fruit and exceptional winter hardiness—what more could anyone ask from a small tree?

Growing

Crabapples prefer **full sun** but tolerate partial shade. The soil should be of **average to rich fertility, moist** and **well drained**. These trees tolerate damp soil but suffer in wet locations.

Tips

Crabapples make excellent specimen plants. Many varieties are quite small, so there is one to suit almost any size of garden. Some forms are even small enough to grow in large containers. The flexibility of the young branches makes these trees good choices for creating espalier specimens.

Recommended

Hundreds of crabapple species, varieties and cultivars are available. One of the most important attributes to look for is disease resistance. Even the most beautiful flowers, fruit or habit will never look good if the plant is ravaged by pests or disease.

Malus cultivars (above & below)

Ask for information about new resistant cultivars at your local nursery or garden center.

Features: attractive spring flowers in shades of white, pink, red or purple-red; late-season and winter fruit; fall color; attractive habit and bark **Habit:** rounded, mounded or spreading, small to medium, deciduous tree
Height: 5–30' **Spread:** 6–30'
Hardiness: zones 4–8

Forsythia
Forsythia

F. x *intermedia* (above & below)

Growing

Most selections grow best in **full sun,** but some prefer **light or partial shade.** The soil should be of **average fertility, moist** and **well drained.** Forsythia is more cold hardy than its flower buds. In a sheltered spot, or if protected by winter snow cover, forsythia may flower in a colder-than-recommended hardiness zone.

Tips

Include forsythia in a shrub or mixed border where other flowering plants will provide interest once forsythia's early-season glory has passed.

Recommended

F. x ***intermedia*** is a large shrub with upright stems that arch as they mature. It grows 5–10' tall and spreads 5–12'. Bright yellow flowers emerge before the leaves in early to mid-spring. Many cultivars are available. A few of the better cultivars include **'Golden Peep,' 'Gold Tide,' 'New Hampshire Gold'** and the variegated selections **'Fiesta'** and **'Kumson.'**

This shrub is treated a bit like relatives. It's fabulous to see when it bursts into bloom after a long, dreary winter, but, once it's done flowering, it just seems to be taking up garden space. However, new selections with more decorative foliage have increased forsythia's appeal.

Forsythia can be used as a hedging plant, but it looks most attractive and flowers best when grown informally, especially in groups of 3–5.

Features: attractive yellow flowers in early to mid-spring **Habit:** spreading, deciduous shrub with upright or arching branches **Height:** 2–10' **Spread:** 3–15' **Hardiness:** zones 5–8

Fothergilla
Fothergilla

Flowers, fragrance, fall color and interesting, soft tan to brownish stems give fothergillas year-round appeal.

Growing
Fothergillas bear the most flowers and have the best fall color in **full sun,** but they also grow well in partial shade. The soil should be of **average fertility, humus rich, acidic, moist** and **well drained.**

Tips
Fothergillas are attractive and useful in shrub or mixed borders, in woodland gardens and when combined with evergreen groundcover.

Recommended
F. gardenii (dwarf fothergilla) is a bushy shrub that bears fragrant, white flowers. The foliage turns yellow, orange and red in fall. It grows 24–36" tall and wide, some-times taller. Cultivars are available. **'Blue Mist'** has bluish foliage throughout the growing season.

F. major (large fothergilla) is a larger, rounded shrub up to 8' tall and 6' wide that bears fragrant, white flowers. The fall colors are yellow, orange and scarlet. **'Blue Shadow'** is an exceptional recent cultivar with attractive blue foliage. **'Mount Airy'** is a smaller selection with dark green foliage that turns shades of yellow, orange and scarlet in fall.

F. major (above & below)

The bottlebrush-shaped flowers of fothergillas have a delicate honey scent. These generally problem-free shrubs make wonderful companions to azaleas, rhododendrons and other acid-loving woodland plants.

Features: fragrant, white spring flowers; fall color **Habit:** dense, rounded or bushy, deciduous shrub **Height:** 2–8' **Spread:** 3–6' **Hardiness:** zones 4–9

Fringe Tree

Chionanthus

C. virginicus (above & below)

Cold hardy and adaptable to a wide range of growing conditions, fringe trees become densely covered in silky white, honey-scented flowers that shimmer in the wind over a long period in spring.

Growing

Fringe trees prefer **full sun**. They do best in soil that is **fertile, acidic, moist** and **well drained** but adapt to most soil conditions. In the wild they are often found growing alongside stream banks.

Tips

Fringe trees begin flowering at a very early age. They work well as specimen plants, as part of a border or beside a water feature.

Recommended

C. retusus (Chinese fringe tree) is a rounded, spreading shrub or small tree with deeply furrowed, peeling bark and erect, fragrant, white flower clusters. (Zones 5–9)

C. virginicus (white fringe tree) is a spreading, small tree or large shrub that bears fragrant, drooping, white flowers.

Features: fragrant, white flowers in early summer; attractive bark **Habit:** rounded or spreading, deciduous, large shrub or small tree **Height:** 10–25' **Spread:** 10–25' **Hardiness:** zones 4–9

Glossy Abelia
Abelia

A. x *grandiflora* (above & below)

This vigorous shrub is one of the few that flowers during summer. It produces an abundance of pink buds and white flowers in late spring and summer, making a wonderful garden display.

Growing

Glossy abelia grows well in **full sun** or **partial shade**. The soil should be **fertile, relatively moist** and **well drained**. Prune this plant right after flowering to keep it full and tidy.

Tips

Glossy abelia makes a lovely addition to a shrub or mixed border. Because it is a relatively large shrub, it is best suited to the back of the border.

Recommended

A. **x** *grandiflora* is a rounded, evergreen or semi-evergreen shrub with arching branches covered in glossy, dark green foliage. Funnel-shaped flowers are borne from mid-summer until fall. The fragrant flowers are white with a hint of pink. Variegated cultivars are also available.

For a wonderfully fragrant spring bouquet, cut some glossy abelia branches just before the flower buds open.

Features: glossy foliage, becoming orange to red in fall; white summer flowers
Habit: rounded to upright, semi-evergreen shrub **Height:** 6–10' **Spread:** 4–6'
Hardiness: zones 4–8

Glossy Privet
Ligustrum

L. japonicum (above)

Glossy privets are among the most used hedge plants of all time throughout the South. Their vigorous and dense growth habit lend well to this application, and they're easily sheared if desired.

Growing
Glossy privets grow equally well in **full sun** or **partial shade**. They adapt to any **well-drained** soil, and they tolerate polluted and urban conditions.

Hedges can be pruned twice each summer. Plants grown in borders or as specimens should be kept neat by removing up to one-third of the mature growth each year.

Tips
Fast-growing, adaptable and inexpensive, glossy privets are commonly grown as hedges. An unpruned privet becomes a large shrub with arching branches that looks quite attractive, especially when in bloom.

Recommended
L. japonicum (Japanese privet) is a dense, compact, evergreen shrub, up to 10–12' tall and 8' wide. The roundish oval leaves have glossy, dark green uppersides and paler undersides. Fragrant, white flower clusters of mid-summer to fall are followed by black fruit. Many cultivars are available. **'Recurvifolium,'** a slower-growing selection with rounded, leathery foliage, has a mature size less than half that of the species.

L. lucidum (waxleaf privet) is a round-headed, evergreen tree that grows 35–40' tall and wide. Often used as a specimen, it has leathery leaves and large, feathery clusters of fragrant flowers and black fruit.

Many glossy privet species bloom in early summer, with fragrance as a bonus, and produce persistent berries in fall.

Features: adaptability; fast, dense growth
Habit: upright or arching, deciduous or semi-evergreen shrub or tree **Height:** 4–40'
Spread: 4–40' **Hardiness:** zones 3–8

Holly

Ilex

ollies vary greatly in shape and size. They can be such delights when placed with full consideration for their needs.

Growing

These plants prefer **full sun** but tolerate partial shade. The soil should be of **average to rich fertility, humus rich** and **moist**. Hollies perform best in acidic soil with a pH of 6.5 or lower. Shelter hollies from winter wind to help prevent the evergreen leaves from drying out. Apply a summer mulch to keep the roots cool and moist.

Tips

Hollies can be used in groups, in woodland gardens and in shrub and mixed borders. They can also be shaped into hedges. Winterberry is good for naturalizing in moist sites.

Recommended

Of the unending supply of hollies, most are worthy of growing in Southern gardens. Consult your local garden center for their recommendations. Here are a few favorites: *I. cornuta* (Chinese holly) is an evergreen shrub or small tree that is very tolerant of excessive heat. *I. hybrids* offer every form, size and special characteristic available, including broadly pyramidal forms, colorful berries, dwarf selections and nearly black

I. cornuta 'Sunrise'

leaves. *I. opaca* (American holly) grows slowly to 40–50' tall. Hundreds of cultivars provide unique qualities. *I. verticillata* (winterberry, winterberry holly) is a deciduous native grown for its explosion of red, orange or yellow fruit that persists beyond fall. *I. vomitoria*, although often used for tall, dense hedges, makes a nice specimen as well.

Features: attractive, glossy, sometimes spiny foliage; fruit; attractive habit **Habit:** erect or spreading, evergreen or deciduous shrub or tree **Height:** 3–50' **Spread:** 3–40' **Hardiness:** zones 3–9

All hollies have male and female flowers on separate plants, and both must be present for the females to set fruit. One male plant adequately pollinates two or three females.

Hydrangea

Hydrangea

H. *quercifolia* (above)
H. *macrophylla* cultivars (below)

Hydrangeas have many attractive qualities, including showy, often long-lasting flowers and glossy, green leaves that may produce beautiful fall colors.

Growing

Hydrangeas grow well in **full sun** or **partial shade,** and some species tolerate full shade. The soil should be of **average to high fertility, humus rich, moist** and **well drained**. These plants perform best in cool, moist conditions. In hot gardens, shade or partial shade reduces leaf and flower scorch.

Tips

Hydrangeas come in many forms and have many uses. They can be included in shrub or mixed borders or grown in containers. They look good as specimens planted in groups or used as informal barriers

Recommended

H. arborescens (smooth hydrangea) is a rounded shrub that flowers well, even in shade. Superior selections include **'Annabelle'** and **'White Dome.'**

H. macrophylla (bigleaf hydrangea, garden hydrangea) is a large, rounded shrub that grows 6–10' tall and wide. It has large, shiny, dark green leaves and lacecap flowerheads of red, blue, pink or white. The many cultivars can have either hortensia or lacecap flowerheads. The species and cultivars bloom on older wood.

H. paniculata (panicle hydrangea) is a spreading to upright, large shrub or small tree with white flowers in late summer and early fall. **'Grandiflora'** (Peegee hydrangea) is a commonly available cultivar. Other excellent selections include **'Limelight,'** **'Little Lamb'** and **'Pink Diamond.'**

H. quercifolia (oakleaf hydrangea) is a mound-forming shrub with attractive cinnamon brown, exfoliating bark and conical clusters of sterile and fertile flowers. The large, oak-like leaves turn bronze to bright red in fall. Some of the lovely cultivars include **'Little Honey,'** **'Pee Wee,'** **'Snowflake'** and **'Snow Queen.'**

Features: attractive flowers in shades of purple, pink, white and blue; decorative foliage and bark **Habit:** deciduous, mounding or spreading shrub or tree **Height:** 3–22' **Spread:** 3–15' **Hardiness:** zones 4–9

Juniper

Juniperus

With all the choices available—from low, creeping plants to upright, pyramidal forms—there may be a juniper in every gardener's future.

Growing

Junipers prefer **full sun** but tolerate light shade. The ideal soil is of **average fertility** and **well drained,** but these plants tolerate most conditions.

Tips

The wide variety of junipers available endless uses. They make prickly barriers and hedges, and they can be used in borders, as specimens or in groups. Large selections can be used to form windbreaks, whereas low-growing ones can be used in rock gardens and as groundcover.

Recommended

Junipers vary from species to species and often within a species. Cultivars are available for all species. *J. chinensis* (Chinese juniper) is a conical tree or spreading shrub. *J. conferta* and *J. horizontalis* (creeping juniper) are prostrate, creeping groundcovers. *J. davurica* and *J. procumbens* (Japanese garden juniper) are both wide-spreading, stiff-branched, low shrubs. *J. scopulorum* (Rocky Mountain juniper) can be upright, rounded, weeping or spreading. *J. squamata* (singleseed juniper) forms a prostrate or low, spreading

J. squamata 'Blue Arrow' (above)
J. conferta 'Emerald Sea' (below)

shrub or a small, upright tree. *J. virginiana* (eastern redcedar) is a durable, upright or wide-spreading tree.

To avoid a possible rash, wear long sleeves and gloves when handling junipers.

Features: evergreen **Habit:** conical or columnar tree, rounded or spreading shrub or prostrate groundcover **Height:** 4"–80' **Spread:** 18"–25' **Hardiness:** zones 3–9

Leyland Cypress

x Cupressocyparis

x *C. leylandii*

Growing

Leyland cypress prefers **full sun** in open locations but tolerates partial shade. **Moist, well-drained** soils are best.

Tips

Although often used in evergreen privacy screens, Leyland cypress is equally stunning and useful when planted as single specimens or small groupings to create a more naturalistic setting.

Recommended

x *C. leylandii* is the result of crossing *Cupressus macrocarpa* (cypress) and *Chamaecyparis nootkatensis* (false cypress). This hybrid evergreen closely resembles both parents, displaying the best attributes of each genus. It can grow 60–70' tall and 15–20' wide but is often topped or pruned to keep its tall form in check. The long, slender branches grow upright, clothed in flattened, gray-green foliage sprays. Smaller selections are also available in a columnar form.

Leyland cypress has been overused in parts of the South. For the long-term good of this tree, plant it only in a neighborhood with few specimens or none.

Immediately upon mention of the name, Leyland cypress evokes visions of evergreen privacy screening. Introduced in the mid-1970s, this tree has carved out a deep niche in the Tennessee landscape.

Features: evergreen foliage; attractive habit; versatility **Habit:** tall, dense, evergreen, coniferous tree **Height:** 20–70' **Spread:** 6–20 **Hardiness:** zones 6–9

Loropetalum
Chinese Fringe-Flower
Loropetalum

Loropetalum is an attractive spring-flowering shrub that can be used almost anywhere a shrub is needed or wanted. The varieties with reddish purple leaves are a knockout!

Growing

Loropetalum grows almost equally well in **full sun, partial shade** or **light shade.** The ideal soil is **acidic, moist** and **well-drained,** with a **lot of organic matter** mixed in, but loropetalum adapts to sandy or clay soils. This plant is prettiest left unpruned.

Tips

Loropetalum can be used in a wide variety of shrub or mixed beds and borders. The evergreen foliage makes a nice background for other flowering plants.

Recommended

L. chinense is a fast-growing, irregular, rounded to upright shrub with glossy, dark green, evergreen foliage and fragrant, creamy white flowers.

L. chinense cultivar (above & below)

Consider one of the excellent selections with reddish purple leaves and pink flowers, such as **'Razzleberri,' 'Sizzling Pink'** or **'Zhuzhou Fuchsia,'** which has nearly black foliage.

Don't worry if a cold snap appears to have killed your loropetalum; it will regrow from the roots.

Features: spring flowers in various shades of pink and white; attractive foliage; low maintenance **Habit:** low-growing, spreading, evergreen shrub **Height:** 4–6' **Spread:** 4–6' **Hardiness:** zones 5–9

Magnolia

Magnolia

M. *grandiflora* cultivar (above)
M. x *soulangeana* (below)

Magnolias are beautiful, fragrant, versatile plants that also provide attractive winter structure.

Growing

Magnolias grow well in **full sun** or **partial shade**. The soil should be **fertile, humus-rich, acidic, moist** and **well drained**. A summer mulch helps keep the roots cool and the soil moist.

Tips

Magnolias are often used as specimen trees. Small selections can be used in borders.

Avoid planting magnolias where the morning sun will encourage the blooms to open too early in the season, making them vulnerable to cold, wind and rain.

Recommended

Magnolias come in many species, hybrids and cultivars, in a range of sizes and with differing flowering times and flower colors. Check with your local nursery or garden center for availability. Below are some favorites.

M. grandiflora (southern magnolia) is a classic evergreen tree form up to 60' tall.

M. **hybrids** are often deciduous and plentiful, in almost any form and color imaginable. *M.* **Little Girl hybrids** are a fine example of what's available. This late-flowering group includes the selections **'Ann,' 'Betty,' 'Jane,' 'Judy,' 'Randy,' 'Ricki'** and **'Susan.'**

M. x soulangeana (saucer magnolia) is a rounded, spreading, deciduous shrub or tree with pink, purple or white flowers.

M. stellata (star magnolia), a compact, bushy or spreading, deciduous shrub or small tree with fragrant, many-petaled white flowers.

Features: white, pink, purple, yellow, cream or apricot flowers; decorative fruit; attractive foliage, bark and habit **Habit:** upright to spreading, deciduous or evergreen shrub or tree **Height:** 8–70' **Spread:** 5–30' **Hardiness:** zones 4–8

Maple
Acer

Maples are attractive year-round, with delicate flowers in spring, attractive foliage and hanging samaras in summer, vibrant leaf color in fall and interesting bark and branch structures in winter.

Growing

Most maple species do well in **full sun** or **light shade**. The soil should be **fertile, high in organic matter, moist** and **well drained**.

Tips

Maples can be used as specimen trees, as large elements in shrub or mixed borders or as hedges. Some are useful as understory plants bordering wooded areas; others can be grown in containers on patios or terraces. Few Japanese gardens are without one or more of the attractive small selections. Almost all maples can be used to create bonsai specimens.

Recommended

Maples are among the most popular shade and street trees. Many are very large when fully mature, but a few small species are useful in small gardens, including *A. campestre* (hedge maple), *A. ginnala* (amur maple), *A. griseum* (paperbark maple), *A. japonicum* (full-moon maple), *A. palmatum* (Japanese maple) and *A. rubrum* (red maple). A vast array of unique

A. rubrum (above), *A. palmatum* cultivar (below)

cultivars are available. Check with your local nursery or garden center for availability.

Features: attractive foliage, bark and form; fall color; greenish yellow flowers; winged fruit **Habit:** small, multi-stemmed, deciduous tree or large shrub **Height:** 6–80' **Spread:** 6–70' **Hardiness:** zones 2–8

Nandina • Heavenly Bamboo

Nandina

N. domestica 'Fire Power' (above)
N. domestica 'Compacta' (below)

A staple in the South, nandina has even been scorned because of its ease of growth. This lovely shrub is extremely drought tolerant, unaffected by pollution and flourishes almost anywhere. It is well suited to any type of setting.

Growing

Nandina prefers **full sun** or **partial shade** in **humus-rich, moist, well-drained** soil. It is prone to chlorosis when planted in alkaline soils.

It prefers regular water but can tolerate drier conditions. Shrubs in full sun that experience some frost produce the best fall and winter color.

Tips

Use nandina in shrub borders, as background plants, and as informal hedges and screens. It is a great plant for containers. Mass planting ensures a good quantity of the shiny, bright red berries.

Recommended

N. domestica produces clumps of thin, upright, lightly branched stems and fine-textured foliage. It grows 6–8' tall and 3–5' wide and slowly spreads by suckering. It bears large, loose clusters of small, white flowers followed by persistent, spherical fruit. New foliage is tinged bronze to red, becoming light to medium green in summer, with many varieties turning red to reddish purple in fall and winter. Many colorful, compact and dwarf cultivars are available.

Nandina's colorful berries persist through winter. They attract birds, which then spread the seeds.

Also called: sacred bamboo, common nandina Features: late-spring to early-summer flowers; fruit; decorative foliage; tough and long-lived Habit: upright to rounded, evergreen or semi-evergreen shrub Height: 18"–8' Spread: 18"–5' Hardiness: zones: 7–9

Oak

Quercus

*T*he oak's classic shape, outstanding fall color, deep roots and long life are some of its many assets. Plant it to enjoy its beauty yourself and for posterity.

Growing

Oaks grow well in **full sun** or **partial shade**. The soil should be **fertile, moist** and **well drained**. These trees can be difficult to establish; transplant them only when they are young. Do not disturb the ground around the base of an oak; this tree is very sensitive to changes in grade.

Tips

These large trees are best as specimens or for groves in parks and large gardens.

Recommended

There are many oaks to choose from. Here are a few popular species. **Q. alba** (white oak) is a rounded, spreading tree with peeling bark and purple-red fall color. **Q. coccinea** (scarlet oak) is noted for having the most brilliant red fall color of all the oaks. **Q. laurifolia** (laurel oak) is a rounded tree with ornate bark and narrow, glossy leaves. **Q. palustris** (pin oak), a vigorous, small, conical tree with pendent lower branches and deeply lobed leaves, is suited to small landscapes. **Q. rubra** (red oak) is a rounded, spreading tree with fall color ranging from yellow to red-brown. **Q. virginiana** (live oak) is a massive, wide-spreading tree with reddish brown bark and small, leathery,

Q. virginiana (above & below)

dark green leaves. Some cultivars are available. Check with your local nursery or garden center.

Most acorns are considered inedible. Some kinds can be eaten after they have been processed to leach out the bitter tannins.

Features: attractive foliage and bark; fall color; acorns **Habit:** large, rounded, spreading, deciduous tree **Height:** 35–120' **Spread:** 10–100' **Hardiness:** zones 3–9

Plum Yew

Cephalotaxus

C. harringtonia 'Duke Gardens'

This yew-like shrub offers all of the visual qualities of a yew but tolerates heat better and is much less attractive to deer.

Growing

Plum yews prefer locations in **full sun** or **partial shade**. The soil should be **moist, fertile** and **well drained**. Locations sheltered from wind are best.

Tips

This evergreen shrub is excellent for planting en masse for added impact and thrives in foundation plantings. Plum yews also tolerate hard clipping, making them ideal for hedges. They make fine specimens all on their own but also mix well into borders and beds.

Recommended

C. harringtonia (plum yew, Japanese plum yew) is a coniferous shrub and occasionally a small tree. It bears sharply pointed, slightly curved, needle-like leaves. Cultivars are available in tall upright, low-growing and spreading forms. **'Duke Gardens'** grows only 3–4' tall and wide. **'Fastigiata'** achieves a more upright, columnar form, growing to 10' tall. **'Korean Gold'** produces golden foliage.

This particular Cephalotaxus *species is native to parts of Korea and Japan. Other species hail from northeastern India, Burma, Vietnam, China and Taiwan.*

Features: evergreen foliage; attractive form
Habit: upright and rounded to sprawly, coniferous shrub or small tree **Height:** 2–10'
Spread: 3–10' **Hardiness:** zones 6–9

Prunus

Prunus

*P*runus blossoms are so beautiful and uplifting after the gray days of winter that few gardeners can resist these plants.

Growing

Prunus selections prefer **full sun**. The soil should be of **average fertility, moist** and **well drained**. Shallow roots emerge from the ground if the tree is not getting sufficient water.

Tips

Prunus species are beautiful as specimen plants. Many are small enough for almost any garden. Small selections can be used in borders or grouped to make informal hedges or barriers.

Recommended

Here are a few of the many popular selections available. Check with your local nursery or garden center for other possibilities. *P. caroliniana* (Carolina cherry laurel) is an upright shrub suitable for hedging or training as a small tree. The small, creamy white flowers appear in late winter or early spring. *P. glandulosa* (dwarf flowering almond) is a rounded shrub with white to pale pink flowers. Double-flowering cultivars are available. *P. laurocerasus* (cherry laurel) is a dense, bushy shrub with glossy leaves and fragrant, white flowers. *P. mume* (Japanese flowering apricot) is a spreading, deciduous tree with fragrant, white or pink flowers. Many cultivars bear ruffled, double

P. serrulata 'Kwanzan' (above)

blossoms. *P. 'Okame'* is a bushy tree or shrub with dark green foliage that turns bright orange-red in fall. Carmine red blossoms appear in early spring. *P. serrulata* is a rounded tree with peeling, glossy, copper bark, white spring flowers and great fall color. *P. subhirtella* (Higan cherry) is a rounded or spreading tree with white or light pink flowers, often-attractive bark and bright fall color. **'Autumnalis'** bears semi-double, pink-tinted, white flowers. *P. x yedoensis* (Potomac cherry, Yoshino cherry) is a large, spreading tree with arching branches, dark green leaves and pale pink early-spring flowers. The many cultivars offer varied pink blossoms and weeping habits.

Features: attractive pink or white spring to early-summer flowers; fruit; attractive bark; fall color **Habit:** upright, rounded, spreading or weeping deciduous tree or shrub
Height: 4–75' **Spread:** 4–50'
Hardiness: zones 2–8

Redbud

Cercis

C. canadensis (above & below)

Growing

Redbuds grow well in **full sun, partial shade** or **light shade**. The soil should be a **fertile, deep loam** that is **moist** and **well drained**. Redbuds have tender roots and do not like being transplanted.

Tips

Redbuds can be used as specimen trees, in shrub or mixed borders or in woodland gardens.

Recommended

C. canadensis (eastern redbud) is a spreading, multi-stemmed tree that bears red, purple or pink flowers. Bronze when young, the foliage fades to green over summer and turns bright yellow in fall. The species grows 30' tall and wide. Many beautiful cultivars are available. '**Alba**' bears white blossoms. '**Forest Pansy**' has dramatic dark red-purple leaves.

C. chinensis (Chinese redbud) is a densely branched shrub or small tree with rounded, glossy leaves that turn yellow in fall. Clusters of pink to lavender-pink flowers emerge in spring. This species grows 20' tall and 15' wide. Cultivars are available. '**Avondale**' bears deep purple flowers.

Redbuds are an outstanding treasure of spring. Deep magenta flowers bloom before the leaves emerge, and their impact is intense. As the buds open, the flowers turn pink, covering the long, thin branches in pastel clouds.

Redbuds are not as long-lived as many other trees, so use their delicate beauty to complement more permanent trees.

Features: red, purple or pink spring flowers; fall color **Habit:** rounded or spreading, multi-stemmed, deciduous tree or shrub
Height: 20–30' **Spread:** 15–30'
Hardiness: zones 4–9

Rhododendron • Azalea

Rhododendron

Even without their flowers, rhododendrons are wonderful landscape plants. Their striking, dark green foliage lends an interesting texture to a shrub planting in summer.

Growing

Rhododendrons prefer **partial shade** or **light shade,** but they tolerate full sun in a site with adequate moisture. A location sheltered from strong winds is preferable. The soil should be **fertile, humus-rich, acidic, moist** and **very well drained**. Rhododendrons are sensitive to high pH, salinity and winter injury.

Tips

Use rhododendrons and azaleas in shrub or mixed borders, in woodland gardens, as specimen plants, in group plantings, as hedges or informal barriers, in rock gardens and in planters on a shady patio or balcony.

Rhododendrons and azaleas are generally grouped together. Extensive breeding and hybridizing is making it more and more difficult to label them separately.

Rhododendron translates as 'rose tree'— an apt description of these beautiful plants.

Azalea hybrids (above & below)

Recommended

In our area, we can grow many different rhododendron and azalea species and cultivars. It's difficult to know where to even begin. Many wonderful nurseries and specialty growers can help you find the right rhododendron or azalea for your garden.

Features: late-winter to early-summer flowers in almost every color imaginable; attractive foliage and habit **Habit:** upright, mounding, rounded, evergreen or deciduous shrub
Height: 2–12' **Spread:** 2–12'
Hardiness: zones 3–8

River Birch

Betula

B. nigra (above & below)

When it comes to showy bark, birches are unmatched. As they age, the attractive peeling bark adds a whole new dimension to the garden.

Growing

River birch grows well in **full sun, partial shade** or **light shade**. The soil should be of **average to high fertility, moist** and **fairly well drained**. Periodic flooding is tolerated, but persistently wet soils will kill this tree.

Tips

River birch is often used as a specimen. Its small leaves and open canopy provide light shade that allows perennials, annuals and lawns to flourish beneath. If you have enough space in your garden, river birch looks attractive when grown in groups near natural or artificial water features. Some people consider river birch to be messy, because it sheds thin branches through-out the year.

Recommended

B. nigra (river birch, black birch, red birch) grows 60–90' tall, spreads 40–60' and is resistant to pests and diseases. It has shaggy, cinnamon brown bark that flakes off in sheets when the tree is young, but the bark thickens and becomes more ridged as the tree matures. The cultivar **'Heritage'** is noted for its exceptional peeling bark.

The bark of certain birch species has been used to make canoes, shelters and utensils.

Features: attractive foliage and bark; fall color; winter and spring catkins **Habit:** open, deciduous tree **Height:** 40–90' **Spread:** 30–60' **Hardiness:** zones 3–8

Spirea
Spiraea

Spireas, seen in so many gardens and with dozens of cultivars, remain undeniable favorites. With a wide range of forms, sizes and colors of both foliage and flowers, spireas have many possible landscape uses.

Growing

Spireas prefer **full sun**. The soil should be **fertile, acidic, moist** and **well drained**. To help prevent foliage burn, provide protection from very hot sun.

Tips

Spireas are used in shrub or mixed borders, in rock gardens and as informal screens and hedges.

Recommended

Check with your local nursery or garden center to see which of the many spirea species, cultivars and hybrids are available.

S. japonica is an upright, shrubby species that grows 4–6' tall. It bears 8" wide clusters of pink flowers atop the lush green foliage.

S. nipponica **'Snowmound'** is a compact, spreading shrub that grows only 24–36" tall and wide, with a profusion of white flowers in late spring.

S. prunifolia (bridal wreath spirea) is a large shrub with graceful, arching branches that carry small, double, white flowers from base to tip in early spring.

S. japonica 'Goldmound' (above)
S. x vanhouttei (below)

S. x *vanhouttei* (bridal wreath spirea, Vanhoutte spirea) is a dense, bushy shrub with arching branches that bear clusters of white flowers.

Features: attractive white or pink summer flowers; decorative habit **Habit:** round, bushy, deciduous shrub **Height:** 1–10'
Spread: 1–12' **Hardiness:** zones 3–9

Summersweet
Clethra

C. alnifolia cultivar (above & below)

*Summersweet is useful
in damp, shaded gardens,
where the late-season flowers
are much appreciated.*

Summersweet attracts butterflies and other pollinators. It is one of the best shrubs for adding fragrance to your garden.

Growing

Summersweet grows best in **light or partial shade**. The soil should be **fertile, humus rich, acidic, moist** and **well drained**.

Tips

Although not aggressive, this shrub tends to sucker, forming a colony of stems. Use it in a border or in the light shade along the edge of a woodland garden.

Recommended

C. alnifolia is a large, rounded, upright, colony-forming shrub 3–8' tall and 3–6' wide. Attractive spikes of white flowers are borne in mid- to late summer. The foliage turns yellow in fall. Recommended cultivars include the low-growing **'Hummingbird'** and **'Ruby Spice,'** a selection with reddish pink flowers. **'White Dove'** is a compact selection with white flowers.

Also called: sweet pepperbush, sweetspire
Features: fragrant, white or reddish pink summer flowers; attractive habit; fall color
Habit: rounded, suckering, deciduous shrub
Height: 2–8' **Spread:** 3–8'
Hardiness: zones 3–9

Sweet Gum
Liquidambar

L. styraciflua (above & below)

Always a contender for the best fall color award, this tree has distinctive star-shaped leaves that exhibit a fall riot of yellow, orange, red and purple.

Growing

Sweet gum grows well in **full sun** or **partial shade,** but it develops the best color in full sun. The soil should be of **average fertility, slightly acidic, moist** and **well drained**. This tree needs a lot of room for its roots to develop.

Tips

Sweet gum is attractive as a shade tree, street tree or specimen tree or as part of a woodland garden. The spiny fruit of most selections makes them inappropriate near patios, decks or walkways.

Recommended

L. styraciflua is a neat, symmetrical, pyramidal or rounded tree that grows 60–75' tall and 40–50' wide. Spiny fruits drop off the tree over winter and often as late as the following summer. Corky ridges may develop on young bark but disappear as the tree ages. **'Rotundiloba'** is a fruitless selection. **'Starlight'** is a variegated form.

Features: attractive habit; fall color; spiny fruit; corky bark **Habit:** pyramidal to rounded, deciduous tree **Height:** 50–75'
Spread: 40–50' or more
Hardiness: zones 5–9

Tulip Poplar

Liriodendron

L. tulipifera (above & below)

Tennessee's state tree has, as its common name suggests, tulip-like flowers of greenish yellow and orange and uniquely shaped leaves that are also reminiscent of tulip blossoms.

The genus name Liriodendron *comes from the Greek and means 'lily tree.'*

Growing

Tulip poplar grows well in **full sun** or **partial shade**. The soil should be **average to rich, slightly acidic** and **moist**. This tree needs plenty of room for its roots to grow. It does not tolerate drought. Because tulip poplar is one of the fastest growing trees, it can have weak branches that snap easily in heavy winds.

Tips

This beautiful, massive tree needs a lot of room to grow. Parks, golf courses and large gardens can use this tree as a specimen or in a group planting, but its susceptibility to drought and need for root space make it a poor choice on small properties or as a street tree.

Recommended

L. tulipifera is native to the eastern U.S. It is known more for its unusually shaped leaves than for its tulip-like flowers. The blooms are often borne high in the tree and go unnoticed until the falling petals litter the ground. The foliage turns golden yellow in fall. The fruit is a cone-shaped cluster of long-winged nutlets, green at first and maturing to pale brown. The species can reach 75–100' in height and 30–50' in width. **'Fastigiatum'** ('Arnold') is a columnar selection with a 50–60' mature height and a 20' spread. **'Aureomarginata'** produces leaves with yellow-green margins and grows 70' tall and 30' wide.

Features: early-summer flowers; attractive foliage, fruit and habit **Habit:** large, rounded, oval, deciduous tree **Height:** 50–100' **Spread:** 20–50' **Hardiness:** zones 4–9

Viburnum

Viburnum

Good fall color, attractive form, shade tolerance, scented flowers and attractive fruit put the viburnums in a class by themselves.

Growing

Viburnums grow well in **full sun, partial shade** or **light shade**. The soil should be of **average fertility, moist** and **well drained**. Viburnums tolerate alkaline and acidic soils.

These plants look neatest if deadheaded, but at the cost of the fruit. Fruiting is better when more than one plant of a species is grown.

Tips

Viburnums can be used in borders and woodland gardens. They are a good choice for plantings near swimming pools.

Recommended

Many viburnum species, hybrids and cultivars are available. *V. carlesii* (Korean spice viburnum) is a dense, bushy, rounded, deciduous shrub with white or pink, spicy-scented flowers (zones 5–8); *V. dentatum* (arrow-wood) is a shade-loving, upright shrub with blue fruit. (Zones 3–7) *V. opulus* (European cranberrybush, Guelder-rose) is a rounded, spreading, deciduous shrub with lacy-looking flower

V. plicatum var. *tomentosum* 'Mariesii' (above)
V. plicatum var. *tomentosum* (below)

clusters. (Zones 3–8) *V. plicatum* var. *tomentosum* (doublefile viburnum) has a graceful, horizontal branching pattern, which gives the shrub a layered effect, and lacy-looking, white flower clusters. (Zones 5–8) *V. trilobum* (American cranberrybush, highbush cranberry) is a dense, rounded shrub with clusters of white flowers and edible, red fruit. (Zones 2–7)

Features: possibly fragrant, attractive white or pink flowers; attractive foliage; fall color; fruit **Habit:** bushy or spreading, evergreen, semi-evergreen or deciduous shrub **Height:** 18"–20' **Spread:** 18"–15' **Hardiness:** zones 2–8

Weigela
Weigela

W. florida 'Variegata' (above)
W. florida cultivar (below)

Growing

Weigela prefers **full sun** but tolerates partial shade. The soil should be **fertile** and **well drained**. This plant adapts to most well-drained soil conditions.

Tips

Weigela can be used in shrub or mixed borders, in open woodland gardens and as informal barrier plantings. Some of the prettiest plants are those not pruned but left to their natural form.

Recommended

W. florida is a spreading shrub with arching branches that bear clusters of dark pink flowers. Many hybrids and cultivars are available. **'Carnival'** has thick, azalea-like flowers in red, white or pink. **'Midnight Wine'** is a low-mounding dwarf with dark burgundy foliage. **'Polka'** has bright pink flowers. **'Red Prince'** bears dark red flowers. **'Rubidor'** produces yellow foliage and red flowers. **'Variegata'** has variegated, yellow-green foliage and pink flowers. **'Wine and Roses'** bears dark burgundy foliage and rosy pink flowers.

Weigela has been improved through breeding, and selections with more compact forms, longer flowering periods and greater cold tolerance are now available.

Weigela is one of the longest-blooming shrubs, with the main flush of blooms lasting as long as six weeks. It often re-blooms if sheared lightly after the first flowers fade.

Features: late-spring to early-summer flowers in shades of red, white or pink; decorative foliage **Habit:** upright or low, spreading, deciduous shrub **Height:** 1–9'
Spread: 1–12' **Hardiness:** zones 3–8

Carefree Beauty
Modern Shrub Rose or Landscape Rose

This magnificent rose was developed by the late Dr. Griffith J. Buck at Iowa State University. It is one in the long line of Dr. Buck's 'prairie' showstoppers that are perfectly suited to Southern gardens.

Growing
Carefree Beauty requires a location in **full sun. Organically rich, slightly acidic, well-drained** soil is best, but this shrub rose can tolerate slight shade and poorer soils.

Tips
This upright shrub's spreading habit makes it an ideal candidate for a low-maintenance hedge. It also makes a fine specimen, and it will complement other flowering shrubs and perennials in mixed borders.

Recommended
Rosa **'Carefree Beauty'** bears small clusters of 4½" wide, semi-double, deep pink blossoms, not once but twice throughout the growing season. The large size of the blossoms compensates for the small number at the end of each stem. The fragrant flowers beautifully complement the smooth, olive green foliage. Orange-red hips add interest from winter until early spring.

'Carefree Beauty' (above)
'Abraham Darby' (below)

Abraham Darby is another fine landscape rose that is well suited to growing in the South. It bears double, apricot yellow blooms infused with pale pink.

Features: fragrant, large, deep pink blossoms; disease-free foliage; vigorous growth habit **Height:** 5–6' **Spread:** 4–5'
Hardiness: zones 3–9

Cupcake
Miniature Rose

'Cupcake' (above), Rise 'n' Shine (below)

Growing
Cupcake grows best in **full sun**. The soil should be **fertile, humus rich, slightly acidic, moist** and **well drained**. Dead-head to keep the plants neat and encourage continuous blooming.

Tips
Miniature roses such as Cupcake are sometimes used as annual bedding plants. As annual or perennial shrubs, they can be included in window boxes, planters and mixed containers. In a bed or border they can be grouped together or planted individually to accentuate specific areas. They can also be planted en masse as groundcover or to create a low hedge.

Recommended
Rosa 'Cupcake' is a compact, bushy shrub with glossy, green foliage that resembles a miniature version of a high-centered, large-flowered modern rose. It produces small clusters of double, pink flowers all summer.

Cupcake has strong, healthy growth and blooms throughout the season. It is a disease-resistant, thornless miniature rose that requires very little maintenance.

Rise 'n' Shine is a popular miniature selection that works beautifully in containers and along the edges of sunny borders. It bears unusual quill-like petals in a hybrid tea form in rosette clusters.

Features: bushy habit; slightly fragrant, early-summer to fall flowers in light to medium pink
Height: 12–18" **Spread:** 12–14"
Hardiness: zones 5–8

Double Delight

Hybrid Tea Rose

*T*he aptly named Double Delight pleases with both its strong, sweet, lightly spicy fragrance and its unique flower color.

Growing

Double Delight prefers **full sun** and **fertile, moist, well-drained** soil with at least **5% organic matter** mixed in. This rose can tolerate light breezes, but keep it out of strong winds. This heavy feeder and drinker does not like to share its root space with other plants.

Blackspot can be a problem for Double Delight. Cool, wet weather can promote mildew.

Tips

It's sometimes difficult to find a place in a bed or border for this unique flower color, which best complements solid, deep, dark red or creamy white flowers in mixed beds in monochromatic schemes.

Try planting this rose in a warm, dry location or in a container where it can be easily monitored for disease.

Recommended

Rosa **'Double Delight'** is an upright, irregularly branched plant with medium green foliage. Its fragrance is unaffected by temperature, light or age. The fully double, high-centered flowers open cream with red edges and gradually darken to solid red. Heat intensifies the color.

'Double Delight' (above), 'Just Joey' (below)

Just Joey is one of the most amazing hybrid tea roses. The fully double, coppery soft brown blossoms with buff pink hues have a richness of flower color second to none. Each petal is lightly serrated and wavy along the edges, resulting in a perfectly rounded form.

Also called: Andeli **Features:** fragrant, summer to fall flowers in cream with carmine red edges; repeat blooming **Height:** 3–4' **Spread:** 24–36" **Hardiness:** zones 6–9

Graham Thomas

English Rose or Austin Rose

'Graham Thomas' (above), 'Evelyn' (below)

Well suited to the Tennessee landscape, English roses are distinct from other roses. Their delicate exterior often disguises their tough disposition and willingness to thrive.

Growing

This rose prefers **full sun** but can tolerate slight shade. The soil should be **organically rich, moist** and **well drained**. Deadheading may be required to extend the prolific blooming cycle. Wet weather doesn't trouble this rose, but do not plant it in areas that may be too hot, because the heat reduces flowering and fades the flower color.

Tips

In warm parts of the state, this extremely vigorous rose reaches greater heights if supported, developing into a pillar style or climbing rose. If desired, light pruning keeps Graham Thomas a little smaller.

Recommended

Rosa **'Graham Thomas'** is a very dense, upright shrub with abundant light green leaves. It bears beautiful apricot pink buds that open into large, golden yellow blooms. Carrying up to 35 petals and fading gracefully over time, the double blooms remain cupped until the petals fall cleanly from the plant. This repeat bloomer begins its first prolific cycle in early summer. There are many other English roses to choose from, ranging in color from pink to antique white, apricot and yellow. Consult your local garden center for their recommendations.

Evelyn is one of the many other stunning Austin or English roses available. It bears huge, fully double, shallow-cupped rosettes in shades of pale apricot. The blooms are muddled in their centers, showcasing the yellow base of each petal.

Also called: English Yellow, Graham Stuart Thomas **Features:** strong scented, 4–5" wide flowers in rich, pure yellow; attractive form **Height:** 3½"–7' **Spread:** 4–5' **Hardiness:** zones 6–9

Iceberg
Floribunda Rose

'Iceberg' (above), 'Betty Boop' (below)

Over 40 years have passed since this exceptional rose was first introduced into commerce, and its continued popularity proves it can stand the test of time.

Growing

Iceberg grows best in **full sun**. The soil should be **fertile, humus rich, slightly acidic, moist** and **well drained**. Winter protection is required. Deadhead to prolong blooming.

Tips

Iceberg is a popular addition to mixed borders and beds, and it also works well as a specimen. Plant it in a well-used area or near a window, where its flower fragrance can best be enjoyed. This rose can also be included in large planters or patio containers.

Recommended

Rosa 'Iceberg' is a vigorous shrub with a rounded, bushy habit and light green foliage. It produces clusters of semi-double flowers in several flushes from early summer to fall. A climbing variation of this rose is reputed to be the best climbing white rose ever developed.

Betty Boop is another fine floribunda rose. It bears semi-double, creamy white flowers with carmine edges and pale yellow centers.

Also called: Fée des Neiges
Features: bushy habit; strong, sweet fragrance; early-summer to fall flowers in white, sometimes flushed with pink during cool or wet weather **Height:** 3–4' **Spread:** 3–4' **Hardiness:** zones 5–8

Knockout

Modern Shrub Rose or Landscape Rose

'Knockout' (above), 'The Fairy' (below)

Knockout is simply one of the best new shrub roses to hit the market in years.

The Fairy is another well-known modern shrub rose. It can be used as a groundcover or left to trail over a low wall or embankment. It bears dainty, baby pink rosettes that develop into large clusters perched atop the leaves.

Growing

Knockout grows best in **full sun**. The soil should be **fertile, humus rich, slightly acidic, moist** and **well drained**. This rose blooms most prolifically in warm weather but has deeper red flowers in cooler weather. Deadhead lightly to keep the plant tidy and to encourage prolific blooming.

Tips

This vigorous rose makes a good addition to a mixed bed or border, and it is attractive when planted in groups of three or more. It can be mass planted to create a large display or grown singly as an equally beautiful specimen.

Recommended

Rosa 'Knockout' has a lovely, rounded form with glossy, green leaves that turn to shades of burgundy in fall. The bright, cherry red flowers, in clusters of 3–15, are borne almost all summer and in early fall. Orange-red hips last well into winter. Available cultivars include a light pink selection called **'Blushing Knockout,'** as well as **'Double Knockout'** and **'Pink Knockout.'** All have excellent disease resistance.

Features: rounded habit; light, tea rose–scented, mid-summer to fall flowers in shades of pink and red; disease resistant **Height:** 3–4' **Spread:** 3–4' **Hardiness:** zones 4–10

Lady Banks Rose

Species Rose

*I*t is almost hard to believe your eyes when you first see a mature specimen left to its own devices. Blooming only once, this rose bears a staggering quantity of flowers over a six-week period beginning in very early spring.

Growing

Lady Banks rose thrives and blooms prolifically in **full to partial shade**. The soil should be **moderately fertile, humus-rich, moist** and **very well drained**. Once flowering ends, prune out the spent wood. Ardent pruning and discipline are often required to keep this plant to a reasonable size. The flowers are produced on second- or third-year wood.

Tips

The best place to let this rose 'go wild' is beside an old tree, outbuilding or other strong support. Just bear in mind that there have been stories of sheds collapsing under its weight.

Recommended

Rosa banksiae is a climbing species rose that produces long, slender stems with few or no prickles and pale green foliage. It bears clusters of scented, double, white flowers. Of the cultivars, **'Lutea'** is the most popular; it bears fully double, yellow blossoms.

R. banksiae 'Lutea'

Many astonishing claims have been made about this species rose, and at least one holds true. **Lady Banks** *rose not only holds its own with wisteria but, unlike most roses, blooms at the same time.*

Features: lightly scented, white or yellow flowers; climbing habit **Height:** 15–20'
Spread: 15–20' **Hardiness:** zones 5–10

New Dawn

Climbing Rose

'New Dawn' (above), 'Handel' (below)

Introduced in 1930, New Dawn is still a favorite climbing rose of gardeners and rosarians alike.

Growing

New Dawn grows best in **full sun**. The soil should be **average to fertile, humus rich, slightly acidic, moist** and **well drained**. This rose is disease resistant.

Handel is another climbing rose that loves the heat of the South. It bears semi-double, white to creamy blossoms edged in deep pink.

Tips

Train New Dawn to climb pergolas, walls, pillars, arbors, trellises and fences. With some judicious pruning this rose can be trained to form a bushy shrub or hedge. Plant it where the summer-long profusion of blooms will welcome visitors to your home.

Recommended

Rosa 'New Dawn' is a vigorous climber with upright, arching canes and glossy, green foliage. Singly or in small clusters, it bears pale pink flowers.

Features: glossy, green foliage; climbing habit; long blooming period; pale pearl pink flowers with sweet, apple-like fragrance
Height: 10–15' **Spread:** 10–15'
Hardiness: zones 4–9

Old Blush

Old Garden Rose

'Old Blush' (above), *R. gallica versicolor* (below)

Old Blush is not only beautiful and useful, but it shares a wonderful past along with three other roses brought to Europe from China in the mid-1700s. And the rest is history, as they say.

Growing

Old Blush grows well in **full sun** or **partial shade**. The soil should be **fertile, humus rich** and **well drained**.

Tips

This small rose bush looks stunning toward the front of a mixed shrub border or within a rose garden. The sweet pea–scented blossoms are best enjoyed near pathways, balconies, patios and windows.

Recommended

Rosa **'Old Blush'** is an upright, bushy shrub with a moderately vigorous growth habit. This China rose is resistant to disease and produces smooth canes with few thorns. The smooth, glossy leaves are abundant. Semi-double to double, medium pink blossoms are produced continually from summer to winter.

R. gallica officinalis *and* **R. g. versicolor** *are two additional old garden rose selections that are sure to please. The first bears semi-double, solid purple-pink blooms with bright yellow centers. The latter produces blossoms striped with magenta and white.*

Also called: Common Blush China, Monthly Rose, Parson's Pink China **Features:** lightly fragrant, pink flowers; disease resistant **Height:** 3–4' **Spread:** 36" **Hardiness:** zones 7–9

Queen Elizabeth

Grandiflora Rose

'Queen Elizabeth' (above & below)

The grandiflora classification was originally created to accommodate this rose. Queen Elizabeth is one of the most widely grown and best-loved roses.

Growing

Queen Elizabeth grows best in **full sun**. The soil should be **average to fertile, humus rich, slightly acidic, moist** and **well drained,** but this durable rose adapts to most soils and tolerates high heat and humidity. In spring, prune the plants back to 5–7 canes, each with 5–7 buds.

Tips

Queen Elizabeth is a trouble-free rose that makes a good addition to mixed borders and beds. It can also be used as a specimen, to form a hedge or in a large planter. Its flowers are borne on sturdy stems that make them useful for floral arrangements.

Recommended

Rosa 'Queen Elizabeth' is a bushy shrub with glossy, dark green foliage and dark stems. The cup-shaped, double, pink flowers may be borne singly or in small clusters.

Queen Elizabeth has won many honors and was named World's Favorite Rose in 1979.

Features: glossy, dark green, disease-resistant foliage; lightly scented, soft, pearly pink flowers from summer to fall
Height: 4–6' **Spread:** 30–36"
Hardiness: zones 5–9

Carolina Jessamine

Gelsemium

Most Tennesseans are familiar with this flowering vine. It's known to scamper up large trees, fences and even utility poles. Golden yellow flowers adorn this sprawling vine in late winter, reminding us that spring is just around the corner.

Growing

Carolina jessamine thrives in locations with **full sun;** in partial shade it produces fewer flowers. The soil should be **fertile, moist** and **well drained**.

Pinch the new growth back to encourage a denser growth habit. When the growth thins at the bottom and becomes top heavy, cut the plant back to approximately 24–36" high.

Tips

This vine can be grown on a decorative trellis, pergola or arbor. It is often used to adorn mailboxes and just about anything that requires a bit of color and a vertical element.

All parts of this plant are poisonous.

Recommended

G. sempervirens is a vigorous vine that twines without the aid of tendrils. Masses of fragrant, funnel-shaped flowers in shades of golden to pale yellow are borne in late winter. These brightly colored blossoms perfectly complement the dark glossy foliage and rich brown stems.

G. sempervirens (above & below)

Carolina jessamine can also be used as an effective groundcover. It does best when planted in a place where it can be left to roam and won't be bothered once established.

Features: bright yellow flower clusters; lush foliage; attractive habit **Height:** 15–20'
Spread: 4–5' **Hardiness:** zones 7–9

Chinese Trumpet Vine Trumpet Creeper

Campsis

C. radicans (above & below)

A Chinese trumpet vine is a chugging locomotive of a plant that can cover almost any structure in under five years.

Growing

These heat-tolerant vines flower best in **full sun** but also grow well in partial shade or light shade. Growth is most rampant in **fertile** soil, but any soil will do.

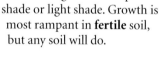

Tips

Chinese trumpet vines cling to any surface—a wall, a tree, a fence or a telephone pole. Once you have one of these endearing and aggressive vines, you'll probably never get rid of it. One plant can provide a privacy screen very quickly, or it can be grown up an exterior wall or over the porch of a house. Chinese trumpet vines can be used on arbors and trellises but need frequent pruning to stay attractive and within bounds. Note that the aerial rootlets can damage painted surfaces.

Recommended

C. grandiflora is not as vigorous or large as *C. radicans*, but the blossoms are larger and a deeper red in color. This species can grow up to 30'. Cultivars with peach flowers are available.

C. radicans is a fast-growing, deciduous vine that climbs by aerial rootlets and bears trumpet-shaped, dark orange flowers for a long period in summer. It spreads by suckers and can form large, thick colonies. **'Crimson Trumpet'** has bright red flowers. **'Flava'** bears yellow flowers.

Hummingbirds are attracted to the long, tube-like flowers of Chinese trumpet vine.

Also called: trumpet vine, hummingbird vine
Features: clinging habit; orange, red or yellow flowers; easy to grow **Height:** 30–40'
Spread: 30–40' **Hardiness:** zones 4–9

Clematis

Clematis

Clematis vines are available with a wide range of blooming times, so it is possible to have clematis in bloom all season.

Growing

Clematis plants prefer **full sun** but tolerate partial shade. The soil should be **fertile, humus rich, moist** and **well drained**. These vines enjoy warm, sunny weather, but the roots prefer to be cool. A thick layer of mulch or a planting of low, shade-providing perennials protects the tender roots. The rootball should be planted about 2" beneath the surface of the soil. Clematis are quite cold hardy but fare best when protected from winter wind.

Tips

Clematis vines can climb up structures such as trellises, railings, fences and arbors. They can also be allowed to grow over shrubs and up trees and can be used as groundcover.

Recommended

Many clematis species, hybrids and cultivars are available, with a wide range of flower forms and colors, blooming times and plant sizes. Check with your local garden center to see what is available.

'Hagley Hybrid' (above)
'Gravetye Beauty' (below)

Plant two clematis varieties that bloom at the same time to provide a mix of color and texture.

Features: twining habit; early- to late-summer flowers in blue, purple, pink, yellow, red or white; decorative seedheads **Height:** 10–17' or more **Spread:** 5' or more
Hardiness: zones 3–8

Climbing Hydrangea

Hydrangea

H. anomala subsp. *petiolaris* (above & below)

Climbing hydrangea is an attractive, pest-free vine that is a great choice to allow to grow up through a tree. The tree provides a structure to climb, and its foliage helps shade the vine.

Growing

Climbing hydrangea grows best in **partial shade** in **acidic, humus-rich, moist, well-drained** soil of **average fertility**. It adapts to full sun and to most moist soils. This vine appreciates **shelter** from the hot sun and from strong or drying winds.

Once established, prune out overly aggressive growth.

Tips

Climbing hydrangea is useful as a climbing vine and as a groundcover. It clings to structures, and it tends to stay flat when grown on surfaces such as walls. It slowly covers walls, and arbors, and truly anything it is near.

Recommended

H. anomala subsp. *petiolaris* is a vigorous, woody climber. The stems cling by aerial roots or holdfasts. The foliage is reminiscent of other hydrangea species and the flower clusters are very similar in appearance to *H. macrophylla*, with flattened clusters of insignificant fertile flowers surrounded by open infertile flowers in creamy white.

The lacecap flower cluster or inflorescence of climbing hydrangea can grow 6–10" in width.

Features: attractive foliage; white summer flowers; clinging habit **Height:** 60–80' or more when climbing; shrubby and sprawling without support **Spread:** dependent on support **Hardiness:** zones 5–9

Cross Vine
Bignonia

*T*his native vine is known to grow very large and at a rapid rate. It blooms like crazy and will disguise unsightly surfaces and structures in no time.

Growing
Cross vine prefers **full sun;** it generally flowers less in partial shade. It favors **organically rich, well-drained** soil but tolerates a wide range of soil conditions.

Prune after flowering or to train the vine on its support.

Tips
This twining plant can climb up just about anything by using the holdfast disks (little suction cup–like bits) at the ends of its tendrils and rootlets. When first planted, it needs to be attached to the surface or structure it will eventually climb. Any type of garden structure or a stone or brick wall, fence, pole or sturdy tree can be used.

Recommended
B. capreolata is a vigorous twining vine that produces lush green foliage along long, tough stems. Tubular, orange-yellow flowers with reddish throats emerge in spring and early summer. The foliage takes on a purplish red coloration as the days grow cooler in winter. Cultivars are available in other fiery colors as well.

B. capreolata

Cross vine is sometimes confused with Chinese trumpet vine. Although they look somewhat similar, cross vine is not as aggressive and blooms at a different time.

Features: flowers with bright, fiery colors; vigorous twining habit **Height:** 30–50'
Spread: 20–40' **Hardiness:** zones 6–9

Five-leaf Akebia

Akebia

A. quinata (above & below)

This vigorous vine twines up anything that gets in its way. It can become invasive, so keep the pruning shears handy if you plan to sit near it.

Growing

Five-leaf akebia grows equally well in **full sun, light shade** or **partial shade,** in soil of **average to high fertility** that is **well drained**. It tolerates full shade and either dry or moist soils.

Tips

Although the fragrant flowers and fruit of this vine are interesting, it is worth growing for the foliage alone.

Five-leaf akebia can quickly cover any sturdy structure, such as a porch railing, trellis, pergola, arbor or fence. Cut the plant back as much and as often as needed to keep it under control. Prune off the fruits to diminish self-seeding.

Recommended

A. quinata is a fast-growing, twining, deciduous climber. In spring, the purple-tinged foliage matures to an attractive blue-green. The deep purple spring flowers are followed by sausage-like fruit pods. **'Alba'** bears white flowers and fruit.

This fragrant-flowered vine can quickly provide privacy and shade when grown over a chain-link fence or on a trellis next to a porch.

Features: attractive foliage; twining habit; purple or white spring flowers; fruit
Height: 20–40' **Spread:** 20–40'
Hardiness: zones 5–8

Japanese Honeysuckle

Lonicera

Honeysuckle vines in general can be rampant and twining, but with careful consideration and placement they won't overrun your garden. The fragrance of the flowers makes any effort worthwhile.

Growing

Honeysuckle vines grow well in **full sun** or **partial shade**. The soil should be **average to fertile, humus rich, moist** and **well drained**.

Tips

These plants can be trained to grow up a trellis, fence, arbor or other structure. Placed in a large container near a porch, a plant will ramble over the edges of the pot and up the railings with reckless abandon.

Recommended

Honeysuckles in general are available in dozens of species, hybrids and cultivars. Check with your local garden center to see what is available.

L. japonica (Japanese honeysuckle) is a vigorous, woody climber with deeply lobed leaves and fragrant, tubular, white flowers with a touch of purple. The flowers eventually change to a pale shade of yellow or cream and are followed by blue-black berries. This species can grow up to 30' in height. Many cultivars and varieties offer variegated foliage and colorful flowers.

L. sempervirens (above)
L. x brownii 'Dropmore Scarlet' (below)

L. sempervirens (trumpet honeysuckle, coral honeysuckle) bears orange or red flowers in late spring and early summer. Many cultivars and hybrids are available, with flowers in yellow, red or scarlet.

L. x brownii 'Dropmore Scarlet,' one of the hardiest of the climbing honeysuckles, is cold hardy to zone 4. It bears bright red flowers for most of summer.

Features: late-spring and early-summer flowers in creamy white, yellow, orange, red or scarlet; twining habit; fruit **Height:** 6–20' **Spread:** 6–20' **Hardiness:** zones 4–9

Ipomoea

Ipomoea

I. batatas 'Blackie' (above), *I. tricolor* (below)

Vines within this group are incredibly easy to grow and are bound to make even the beginner feel like an expert.

Growing

Grow any type of *Ipomoea* vine in **full sun**. A **light, well-drained** soil of **poor fertility** is preferred, but any soil type is tolerated. Soak the seeds for 24 hours before sowing. Start them in individual peat pots if sowing indoors. Plant out in late spring.

Tips

Sweet potato vine is a great addition to mixed planters, window boxes and hanging baskets.

In a rock garden, it will scramble about. Planted along the top of a retaining wall, it will cascade over the edge.

Morning glory and moon vine will embellish a chain-link fence, a wire topiary structure or any object thin enough to twine their tendrils around. Once established, stand back, because these vines grow fast. As ground-covers, they can cover any obstacles they encounter.

Recommended

I. alba (moon vine, moonflower) has sweet-scented, white flowers that open at night. *I. batatas* (sweet potato vine) is a twining climber grown for its attractive foliage rather than its flowers. Several cultivars are available. *I. lobata* (firecracker vine, Spanish flag; *Mina lobata*) is a perennial vine that is often grown as an annual. It bears crimson-flushed stems and stalks clothed in toothed, deeply lobed, green leaves. The tubular flowers emerge in shades of scarlet red but mature to a pale yellow. This species can reach 6–15' in height. Cultivars are available with flowers in shades of yellow to cream. *I. purpurea* (common morning glory) bears trumpet-shaped flowers in purple, blue, pink or white. *I. tricolor* (morning glory) produces purple or blue flowers with white centers. Many cultivars are available.

Features: decorative, colorful foliage; fast growth; white, blue, pink, purple or variegated flowers **Height:** 1–12' **Spread:** 1–10' **Hardiness:** treat as an annual

Kiwi Vine

Actinidia

Kiwi vine is handsome in its simplicity, and its lush green leaves, vigor and adaptability make it very useful, especially on difficult sites.

Growing

Kiwi vine grows best in **full sun** or **partial shade**. The soil should be **fertile** and **well drained**. This plant requires shelter from strong winds. Until it is established, protect it from cats, because the vine's sap sometimes has a catnip-like effect.

The foliage color is best during cool periods in summer. In warm regions, locations with partial shade are best.

Tips

This vine needs a sturdy structure to twine around. Pergolas, arbors and sufficiently large and sturdy fences provide good support. Given a trellis against a wall, a tree or some other upright structure, a kiwi vine will twine upward all summer. Kiwi vine can be grown in a container if desired.

Kiwi vine can grow uncontrollably. Don't be afraid to prune it back if it gets out of hand. Fruit production can be increased by pruning kiwi vines in the same way as grape vines.

Recommended

A. kolomikta (kiwi vine, variegated kiwi vine) has green leaves strongly variegated with pink and white. It bears white flowers and edible, smooth-skinned, greenish yellow fruit.

A. kolomikta (above)

Because both a male and a female vine must be present for fruit to be produced, the plants are often sold in pairs. The male plant usually has more pronounced leaf variegation.

Features: white early-summer flowers; edible fruit; twining habit **Height:** 15–30' to indefinite **Spread:** 15–30' to indefinite **Hardiness:** zones 3–8

Passion Flower
Passiflora

P. caerulea

Tips
Passion flowers are popular additions to mixed containers and make an unusual focal point near a door or other entryway.

Plants bought in spring will quickly climb trellises and other supports over summer. In cool areas, they can be composted at summer's end or cut back and brought inside to enjoy in a bright room over winter.

The leaves of *P. incarnata* taste like peanut butter. The small, round fruits, although edible, are not very tasty.

Recommended
P. caerulea (blue passion flower) bears unusual, purple-banded, purple-white flowers all summer. The species can reach 30' in height. **'Constance Elliott'** bears fragrant, white flowers with pale blue or white filaments.

P. incarnata (maypops) is a vigorous native climbing vine that can exceed 6' in height, attaching itself to a support with tendrils, as does *P. caerulea*. It produces ornate, deeply lobed foliage and fragrant, bowl-shaped, pale purple to nearly white blossoms with purple-and-white coronas, followed by yellow fruit.

Passion flowers are mesmerizing. Most are native to North America. Grown as annuals in cool parts of Tennessee, these fast-growing woody climbers should thrive for years next to a house without any winter protection in Zone 7 and above.

Growing
Grow passion flowers in **full sun** or **partial shade**. They prefer **moist, well-drained** soil of **average fertility**. Keep them **sheltered** from wind and cold.

Fertilize passion flower sparingly. Too much nitrogen will encourage a lot of foliage but few flowers.

Features: exotic flowers with white or pale pink petals with blue or purple bands; decorative habit; ornate foliage **Height:** 6–30' **Spread:** variable **Hardiness:** zones 6–10

Porcelain Berry

Ampelopsis

This vine has attractive foliage, colorful berries, a reliable and vigorous growth habit and incredible fall color. Finally, a vine that has it all, giving year-round interest.

Growing

Porcelain berry requires **full sun** or **partial shade** in a **moist** but **well-drained** location. Prune after flowering if flowering on the previous year's growth; prune from late winter to spring if flowering on the current year's growth.

Tips

Porcelain berry is ideal for climbing up a trellis or support, arbor or pergola. Because of its vigorous growth habit, this vine can cover a wall, fence or old tree in no time at all.

Recommended

A. brevipedunculata is a vigorous climbing vine. The leaves are large and resemble grape leaves. Clusters of small, green flowers emerge in summer, followed by green berries that change to light blue and finally to purple. '**Elegans**' is a little less vigorous than the species and produces dark green foliage with white and pink mottling.

Porcelain berry is often grown for its attractive foliage, which turns a stunning shade of red and yellow in the cool days of fall.

A. brevipedunculata (above & below)

Features: colorful berry clusters; ornate foliage; climbing habit **Height:** 10–15'
Spread: variable **Hardiness:** zones 5–8

Scarlet Runner Bean

Phaseolus

P. coccineus (above & below)

Scarlet runner bean is both functional and beautiful. It'll scramble up a support in no time at all, blooming throughout the summer months and producing buckets of beans good enough to eat.

Growing

Scarlet runner bean prefers to grow in **full sun** in **fertile, moist, well-drained** soil; provide adequate water.

Tips

This twining climber needs something to climb on, such as a trellis, arbor or post. Attach some form of lattice or netting if you want scarlet runner bean to grow up a fence or building.

Recommended

P. coccineus is a fast-growing, twining vine that grows to a height of 7–9'. It bears clusters of scarlet red flowers in summer. Edible, dark green pods follow flowering. Cultivars with red-and-white bicolored or solid white flowers are available.

This plant is at home in the flower garden as well as the vegetable garden. The edible, dark green pods are tender when young but a little tough with age. Pick the pods just after the flowers fade for best taste in a stir-fry.

Features: scarlet, white or bicolored flowers; twining habit; edible fruit **Height:** 6–8' **Spread:** 8–10' **Hardiness:** treat as an annual

Blackberry Lily

Belamcanda

B. chinensis 'Mixed Colors' (above), *B. chinensis* 'Hello Yellow' (below)

Blackberry lily is a good, all-round perennial with attractive foliage, colorful flowers and interesting fruit. Don't worry that this wonderful plant is short-lived, because it self-seeds enough to keep both you and your friends in plants.

Growing

Blackberry lily grows well in **full sun** or **partial shade**. **Moist, well-drained** soil of **average fertility**, with **a lot of organic matter** mixed in, is best. This plant can adapt to sandy soils and some clay soils if enough organic matter has been added. Plants grown in rich soil may need staking.

Features: bright summer flowers in shades of yellow to orange; fall fruit; attractive foliage; easy to grow **Height:** 24–36"
Spread: 12–18" **Hardiness:** zones 5–9

Blackberry lily can be propagated by dividing the rhizomes in spring, or it can easily be grown from seed.

Tips

Blackberry lily provides a vertical element in mixed beds and borders.

Recommended

B. chinensis forms clumps of sword-shaped, green foliage that is arranged in fans, like that of irises. The clusters of star-shaped, yellow to orange flowers with red or maroon spots are held above the foliage. In fall, the fruit splits open to reveal shiny, black berries.

Caladium
Caladium

C. x *hortulanum* hybrid (above)
C. x *hortulanum* 'Sweetheart' (below)

The midribs and veining of the striking foliage help draw the eye to the smashing leaf colors. If you are searching for bold texture, caladium is a must.

Growing

Caladium prefers **partial to full shade,** although a few sun-tolerant selections are available. Caladium likes **slightly acidic**, **humus-rich**, **moist**, **well-drained** soil.

Caladium can be grown from seed but is best grown from tubers. Start the tubers indoors in soil-less planting mix at a minimum temperature of 70° F. The knobby side of each tuber should face up and be level with the soil surface or just below. Once leafed out, the plants can handle root temperatures as low as 55° F.

Dig the tubers up in fall, after the leaves die back. Clean them and let them dry for a few days. Store in slightly damp peat moss at 55–60° F and plant in spring.

Tips

Caladium brings a tropical feel to your garden. It does very well around water features, in woodland gardens, in the herbaceous border en masse or as specimens, and it is a wonderful container plant.

Caladium may irritate the skin, and eating it causes stomach upset.

Recommended

C. x hortulanum (*C. bicolor*) is native to woodland edges in tropical South America. The often-tufted, arrow-shaped, dark green leaves, each 6–12" long, are variously marked with red, white, pink, green, rose, salmon, silver or bronze.

Also called: elephant's ears, heart-of-Jesus, mother-in-law plant, angel wings
Features: ornate, colorful foliage; attractive habit and form **Height:** 18–24"
Spread: 18–24" **Hardiness:** treat as an annual

Canna

Canna

C. hybrid

C. 'Red King Humbert' (above & below)

T he stunning, dramatic cannas give an exotic flair to any garden.

Growing

Cannas grow best in **full sun** or **partial shade**. The soil should be **fertile, moist** and **well drained**. Plant out in spring once the soil has warmed. To get a head start on the growing season, plants can be started early indoors in containers. Deadhead to prolong blooming.

Tips

Cannas can be grown in a bed or border. They make dramatic specimen plants and can even be included in large planters.

Recommended

A wide range of canna cultivars and hybrids are available, including ones with green, bronzy, purple or yellow-and-green-striped foliage. Dwarf cultivars 18–28" tall are also available.

Canna is a reliable perennial in most of Tennessee, but the rhizomes can be lifted after the foliage is killed back in fall if desired. Clean off any clinging dirt and store them in a cool, frost-free location in slightly moist peat moss. Check them regularly; if they start to sprout, pot them and move them to a bright window until they can be moved outdoors.

Features: decorative foliage; white, red, orange, pink, yellow or bicolored summer flowers **Height:** 18"–6' **Spread:** 20–36" **Hardiness:** zones 7–9; treat as a tender perennial

Crocus

Crocus

C. x *vernus* cultivars (above & below)

These harbingers of spring often appear, as if by magic, in full bloom from beneath the melting snow.

Growing

Crocuses grow well in **full sun or light, dappled shade**. The soil should be of **poor to average fertility, gritty** and **well drained**. The corms are planted about 4" deep in fall. The foliage should be left in place after the plants flower, but it can be cut back once it begins to wither and turn brown in summer.

Tips

Crocuses are almost always planted in groups. Drifts of crocuses can be planted in lawns to provide interest and color while the grass still lies dormant. Postpone mowing until the foliage withers in mid-June. In beds and borders, crocuses can be left to naturalize. Groups of plants will fill in and spread out to provide a bright spring welcome. Plant perennials among the crocuses to fill in the gaps once the crocuses die back.

Recommended

Many crocus species, hybrids and cultivars are available. The most familiar spring-flowering crocus is **C. x *vernus*,** commonly called Dutch crocus. Many cultivars are available, with flowers in shades of purple, yellow, white or bicolored, sometimes with darker veins.

Saffron is obtained from the dried, crushed stigmas of C. sativus. Six plants produce enough spice for one recipe. This fall-blooming plant is hardy to zone 5.

Features: early spring flowers in shades of purple, yellow, white or bicolored
Height: 2–6" **Spread:** 2–4"
Hardiness: zones 3–8

Daffodil

Narcissus

When they think of daffodils, many gardeners automatically think of large, trumpet-shaped, yellow flowers, but these bulbs offer a lot of variety in color, form and size.

Growing

Daffodils grow best in **full sun** or **light, dappled shade**. The soil should be **average to fertile, moist** and **well drained**. Plant the bulbs in fall, 2–8" deep, depending on the size of the bulb. As a guide, measure the bulb from top to bottom and multiply that number by three to know how deeply to plant.

Tips

Daffodils are often planted where they can be left to naturalize, in the light shade beneath a tree or in a woodland garden. In mixed beds and borders, the faded leaves are hidden by the summer foliage of other plants.

Recommended

Many species, hybrids and cultivars of daffodils are available. The flowers range from 1½ to 6" across and can be solitary or borne in clusters. About a dozen flower-form categories have been defined.

The cup in the center of a daffodil is the corona, and the group of petals that surrounds the corona is the perianth.

Features: white, yellow, peach, orange, pink or bicolored spring flowers **Height:** 4–24" **Spread:** 4–12" **Hardiness:** zones 3–9

Dahlia

Dahlia

Dahlia cultivars in cutting bed (above)

The variation in size, shape and color of dahlia flowers is astonishing. You are sure to find at least one of these old-fashioned but popular plants that appeals to you.

Growing

Dahlias prefer **full sun**. The soil should be **fertile**, rich in **organic matter, moist** and **well drained**. Tubers can be purchased and started early

indoors. Deadhead to keep the plants tidy and blooming.

Although dahlias are pretty reliable tender perennials in Tennessee, the tubers can be lifted in fall and stored over winter in slightly moist peat moss. Pot them and keep them in a bright room after they start sprouting in mid- to late winter.

Tips

Dahlias make attractive and colorful additions to a mixed border. The small varieties make good edging plants and the large ones make good alternatives to shrubs and provide excellent cut flowers. Varieties with unusual or interesting flowers make attractive specimen plants.

Recommended

Dahlia hybrids are mostly grown from tubers, but a few can be started from seed. Many hybrids are sold based on flower shape, such as collarette, decorative or peony-flowered. The flowers range in size from 2–12" and are available in many shades. Check with your local garden center to see what is available.

Features: summer to fall flowers in shades of purple, pink, white, yellow, orange, red or bicolored; attractive foliage; bushy habit
Height: 8"–5' **Spread:** 8–18"
Hardiness: tender perennial

Elephant's Ear
Colocasia

Bold foliage is this plant's claim to fame, and bold it is. Few other plants have the same visual impact as this Southern favorite.

Growing

Elephant's ear does well in **full sun** or **partial shade**. The soil should be **very fertile, slightly acidic, moist to wet** and **humus rich**.

When planting the tubers, place them 2" deep and approximately 12–18" apart.

Shelter from strong winds helps prevent the leaves from becoming torn and tattered.

This tender perennial commonly returns each year in Tennessee.

Tips

Elephant's ear is stunning when planted in oversized decorative containers and surrounded by plants that spill over the edges. They're also effective when mixed with narrow or finely leaved plants in mixed beds and borders.

Recommended

C. esculenta is a perennial that bears very large, arrow-shaped, dark green leaves supported by stalks up to 36" long. Flowers rarely appear. Cultivars are available with dark red, purple, light green and blackish purple stalks and veins.

Elephant's ear is a marginal aquatic perennial, which means it grows best in wet situations, such water features and bog gardens.

C. esculenta 'Illustris' (above)
C. esculenta (below)

Features: bold foliage and form   **Height:** 5–8'
Spread: 5–8'   **Hardiness:** zones 7–11

Gladiolus

Gladiolus

Grandiflorus type (above), 'Homecoming' (below)

Plant the corms 4–6" deep in spring, once soil has warmed, or start them early indoors. Plant a few corms each week for about a month to prolong the blooming period.

Tips

Planted in groups in beds and borders, glads make a bold statement. If desired, the corms can be pulled up in fall and stored in damp peat moss in a cool, frost-free location for winter.

Recommended

Gladiolus **hybrids** have flowers that come in almost every imaginable shade, except blue. They are commonly grouped into three classifications. **Grandiflorus** is the best known; from each corm grows a single spike of large, often ruffled flowers. **Nanus**, the hardiest group, survives in zone 3 with protection and produces several spikes of up to seven flowers. **Primulinus** bears a single spike of up to 23 flowers that grow more spaced out than those of the grandiflorus.

Perhaps best known as cut flowers, gladiolus add an air of extravagance to the garden.

Growing

Glads grow best in **full sun** but tolerate partial shade. The soil should be **fertile, humus rich, moist** and **well drained**. The flower spikes may need staking and a sheltered location out of the wind to prevent them from blowing over.

Over 10,000 hybrid cultivars of Gladiolus have been developed.

Features: bold mid- to late-summer flowers in almost any color except blue **Height:** 18"–6' **Spread:** 6–12" **Hardiness:** zone 7; grown as a tender perennial in Tennessee.

Grape Hyacinth
Muscari

Tulips should never be alone to signal the arrival of spring. Grape hyacinth bulbs provide the perfect accompaniment, contrasting beautifully with just about any color combination.

Growing

Grape hyacinth prefers **full sun** or **partial shade**. The soil should be well drained and organically rich.

Tips

Grape hyacinth is great for naturalizing. Plant individual bulbs random distances from one another in your lawn, but don't plan on cutting the grass until the grape hyacinth foliage appears to have died down for the year. Grape hyacinth is also quite beautiful planted alongside perennials tall enough to envelope the tired-looking foliage of the grape hyacinth after it blooms.

Often planted around other bulbs as markers to ensure that they aren't forgotten about and dug up, grape hyacinth has leaves that emerge in fall.

Recommended

M. armeniacum (Armenian grape hyacinth) is the best known species. It produces grass-like foliage and clusters of purple-blue grape-like flowers atop slender, green stems. The flowers emit a strong, musky scent.

Grape hyacinth is a welcome sight in the early months of spring, soon after the first bulbs have emerged.

M. armeniacum (above), M. botryoides (below)

M. botryoides (common grape hyacinth) resembles *M. armeniacum* but is slightly more compact. It is less invasive than other species and naturalizes in a more respectable manner.

M. latifolium (bicolor muscari, giant grape hyacinth, one-leaf hyacinth) is a relatively tall, late-blooming species. It bears broader leaves. Each bicolored flower spike has small, light blue sterile flowers near the tip and darker fertile flowers further down.

Features: grape-like clusters of fragrant flowers; decorative habit **Height:** 6–10"
Spread: 6–8" **Hardiness:** zones 2–8

Iris

Iris

I. germanica hybrid (above)
I. germanica 'Stepping Out' (below)

Irises are steeped in history and lore. The flower color range of bearded irises has often been likened to a rainbow.

Growing

Irises prefer **full sun** but tolerate very light or dappled shade. The soil should be of **average fertility** and **well drained**. Japanese iris and Siberian iris prefer a moist but still well-drained soil.

Divide in late summer or early fall. When dividing bearded iris rhizomes, replant with the flat side of the foliage fan facing the garden.

Deadhead irises to keep them tidy.

Tips

All irises are popular border plants, but crested iris and yellow flag iris are also useful alongside streams or ponds. Dwarf cultivars make attractive additions to rock gardens.

Even the residues left on your hands by handling irises may cause severe internal irritation if ingested, so wash your hands afterward. You may not want to plant them close to places where children like to play.

Recommended

Many iris species and hybrids exist. Check with your local garden center to find out what's available. Among the most popular is the bearded iris, often a hybrid of *I. germanica*. It has the widest range of flower colors. *I. cristata* (crested iris) is a low-growing native of the south that bears multicolored blossoms. *I. pseudoacorus* (yellow flag iris) is a water dweller that can tolerate those wet locations where little else thrives.

The bearded iris is Tennessee's state flower.

Features: spring, summer and sometimes fall flowers in almost every color, including bicolored or multi-colored; attractive foliage **Height:** 4"–4' **Spread:** 6"–4' **Hardiness:** zones 3–10

Lily
Lilium

Decorative clusters of large, richly colored blooms grace these tall plants. By choosing cultivars that flower at different times, you can have lilies blooming all season.

Growing

Lilies grow best in **full sun** but like to have their **roots shaded**. The soil should be rich in **organic matter, fertile, moist** and **well drained**.

Tips

Lilies are often grouped in beds and borders and can be naturalized in woodland gardens and near water features. These plants are narrow but tall; plant at least three plants together to create some volume.

Recommended

The many species, hybrids and cultivars are grouped by type. Visit your local garden center to see what is available. The following are two popular groups of lilies.

Asiatic hybrids bear clusters of flowers in a wide range of colors in early summer or mid-summer.

Oriental hybrids bear clusters of fragrant, large, white, pink or red flowers in mid- or late summer.

Asiatic hybrid (above)
Oriental hybrid 'Stargazer' (below)

Lily bulbs are best planted in fall before the first frost, but they can also be planted in spring if bulbs are available.

Features: early-, mid- or late-season flowers in shades of orange, yellow, peach, pink, purple, red or white **Height:** 2–5' **Spread:** 12" **Hardiness:** zones 4–8

Montbretia • Crocosmia

Crocosmia

C. 'Lucifer' (above & below)

The plants need to be divided every 3–5 years to keep them vigorous and blooming profusely.

Tips

Montbretias look striking when massed in a herbaceous or mixed border. They look good next to a pond, where the brightly colored flowers can be reflected in the water.

Recommended

C. x *crocosmiflora* is a spreading plant with long, strap-like leaves and one-sided spikes of red, orange or yellow flowers in mid- and late summer. **'Citronella'** (golden fleece) bears bright yellow flowers.

C. **'Jenny Bloom'** is a vigorous selection with butter-yellow flowers on 24–36" tall plants.

C. **'Lucifer'** is the hardiest of the bunch and bears bright scarlet red flowers. Hummingbirds will love you for planting it.

The intense colors of montbretias are like beacons in the garden.

Growing

Montbretias prefer **full sun**. The soil should be of **average fertility, humus rich, moist** and **well drained**.

So montbretias' wispy blooms really stand out and don't get lost in the mix, use strong backdrop plants such as variegated ornamental grass.

Features: brightly colored flowers in shades of red, orange or yellow; strap-like foliage
Height: 18"–4' **Spread:** 12–18"
Hardiness: zones 5–8

Snowdrop
Galanthus

When winter has you feeling dull and dreary, let the early-blooming snowdrops bring some much-needed color to your winter garden.

Growing

Snowdrops grow well in **full sun** or **partial shade** in **fertile, humus-rich, moist, well-drained** soil. Do not let the soil dry out in summer.

Tips

Snowdrops work well in beds, borders and rock gardens. For the best effect, snowdrops should always be planted in groups and close to each other. Snowdrops can be planted in the lawn or under deciduous shrubs and trees that provide partial shade in summer. Snowdrops are great for naturalizing in lightly shaded woodlands.

Recommended

The various snowdrop species hybridize easily with each other; many hybrids are available.

G. elwesii (giant snowdrop) has larger flowers and foliage than *G. nivalis* and grows taller. The inner petals are heavily marked with green.

G. nivalis (common snowdrop) is a tiny plant that produces honey-scented, small, nodding, white flowers in mid- to late winter. The inner petals are marked with a green 'V' shape. Cultivars are available, some with double flowers and some with yellow markings instead of green.

G. elwesii with winter aconite (above)
G. nivalis (below)

All parts of snowdrops are poisonous if ingested. Handling the bulbs may irritate sensitive skin.

Features: early-blooming, white flowers; strap-like foliage; easy to grow **Height:** 4–12" **Spread:** 4–6" **Hardiness:** zones 3–8

Tulip
Tulipa

Tulips, with their beautifully colored flowers, are a welcome sight in the first warm days of spring.

Growing

Tulips grow best in **full sun;** in light or partial shade, the flowers tend to bend toward the light. The soil should be **fertile** and **well drained**. Plant the bulbs in fall. Cold-treated bulbs can be planted in spring.

Tips

Tulips provide the best display when mass planted in flowerbeds and borders. They can also be grown in containers and can be forced to bloom early in indoor pots.

Although tulips can repeat bloom, many hybrids perform best if replaced each year. Some species and older cultivars can be naturalized in meadow and wildflower gardens.

Recommended

About 100 species of tulips exist. The thousands of hybrids and cultivars are generally divided into 15 groups, according to bloom time and flower appearance. They come in dozens of shades with many bicolored and multi-colored varieties. For best selection, purchase your tulips in early fall.

For a dramatic show, consider interplanting tulips with winter annuals such as pansies and snapdragons.

When choosing tulip bulbs, remember that bigger bulbs produce bigger blooms.

Features: spring flowers in all colors except blue **Height:** 6–30" **Spread:** 2–8" **Hardiness:** zones 3–8; often grown as annuals

Chamomile
Chamaemelum

C. nobile

You too can grow your own crop of medicinal chamomile for those moments when you need to slow things down and calm your frazzled nerves.

Growing
Chamomile prefers **full sun or light shade. Light, moist, well-drained** soil is best.

Tips
This aromatic perennial is perfectly suited to herb gardens created for medicinal purposes. An attractive plant, it also mixes well into borders but can spread, becoming invasive.

It's often used as a groundcover between stepping stones in pathways, and it is well suited to cottage-garden settings and containers.

Recommended
C. nobile is a mat-forming, stalkless perennial with fragrant, divided foliage. It bears daisy-like flowers in summer. Cultivars are available with double flowers or without flowers.

The flowers should be harvested when they are fully open. Once dried, the flowers can be steeped to make a tea that's often used as a sedative. For generations, this herb has also been used in cosmetics and crafts.

Features: aromatic foliage; daisy-like, white-and-yellow flowers; many uses **Height:** 3–12" **Spread:** 12" **Hardiness:** zones 6–9

Chives

Allium

A. *schoenoprasum* (above & below)

The delicate onion flavor of chives is best enjoyed fresh. Mix chives into dips or sprinkle them on salads and baked potatoes.

Chives spread with reckless abandon as the clumps grow larger and the plants self-seed.

Growing

Chives grow best in **full sun.** The soil should be **fertile, moist** and **well drained,** but chives adapt to most soil conditions. These plants are easy to start from seed, but they do like the soil temperature to stay above 65° F before they germinate, so seeds started directly in the garden are unlikely to sprout before early summer.

Tips

Chives are decorative enough to be included in a mixed or herbaceous border and can be left to naturalize. In an herb garden, chives should be given plenty of space to allow self-seeding.

Recommended

A. *schoenoprasum* forms a clump of bright green, cylindrical leaves. Clusters of pinky purple flowers are produced in early and mid-summer. Varieties with white or pink flowers are available. To prevent invasive reseeding, cut the flower stalks before the seedheads ripen.

A. *tuberosum* (garlic chives, Chinese chives) form a clump of flat, bright green leaves that have a strong garlic flavor. The clusters of white late-summer flowers are great for cut flowers.

Features: attractive foliage and form; white, pink or pinky purple flowers **Height:** 8–24"
Spread: 12" or more **Hardiness:** zones 3–9

Dill

Anethum

Dill leaves and seeds are probably best known for their use as pickling herbs, although they have a wide variety of other culinary uses.

Growing

Dill grows best in **full sun** in a **sheltered** location out of strong winds. The soil should be of **poor to average fertility, moist** and **well drained**. Sow seeds every few weeks in spring and early summer to ensure a regular supply of leaves. Because dill and fennel cross-pollinate, causing the seeds of both plants to lose their distinctive flavors, they should not be grown near each other.

Tips

With its feathery leaves, dill is an attractive addition to a mixed bed or border. It can be included in a vegetable garden but does well in any sunny location. Dill also attracts predatory insects and butterfly caterpillars to the garden.

Recommended

A. **graveolens** forms a clump of feathery foliage. Clusters of yellow flowers are borne at the tops of sturdy stems in summer. The plants tend to flower early in hot or dry conditions. **'Fernleaf'** is a dwarf selection that grows just 18" tall.

A. graveolens (above & below)

Dill turns up frequently in historical records as both a culinary and medicinal herb. It was used by the Egyptians and Romans and is mentioned in the Bible.

Features: edible, feathery foliage; yellow summer flowers; edible seeds
Height: 18"–5' **Spread:** 12" or more
Hardiness: annual

English Lavender
Lavandula

L. angustifolia (above & below)

Lavender has antibacterial and anti-fungal properties, and it gives off a sharp, clean scent. Its essential oil can relax yet energize the nervous system.

Growing

Lavender grows best in **full sun** in **alkaline** soil that is **average to fertile** and **very well drained**. Established plants tolerate heat and drought.

Overwatering drowns lavender plants. They benefit from the enhanced drainage that results from being planted in raised beds or clay containers.

Tips

Lavender is deer resistant, and it can be used as an edging plant and in low hedges. Plant with other drought-tolerant species, such as pinks and thyme.

Recommended

L. angustifolia (English lavender) is an aromatic, bushy subshrub that is often treated as a perennial. It bears spikes of small flowers in shades of violet-blue. Cultivars offer different sizes, with flowers in shades of purple, blue or pink.

Features: fragrant, summer-to-fall flowers in shades of purple, blue or pink; attractive foliage **Height:** 8–36" **Spread:** up to 4' **Hardiness:** zones 5–9

Lemon Balm
Melissa

This lemon-scented and fla-vored herb is indispensable to people who love a touch of lemon in their cooking.

Growing

Lemon balm prefers to grow in **full sun** but grows quite success-fully in dappled shade. The ideal soil is **fertile, moist** and **well drained,** but this plant can toler-ate poor, dry soils.

Removing pieces for use encour-ages dense, vigorous growth. It's best to remove the flowers as they emerge.

Tips

Herb gardens are often the pre-ferred location for this useful perennial, but it also works well as a fragrant filler in containers, mixed beds and borders. Like the closely related mints, lemon balm may spread throughout your gar-den. Granted, lemon balm isn't invasive, but it may be best to prevent it from straying.

Recommended

M. officinalis is a bushy, dense-growing perennial with roughly textured, hairy leaves that are fra-grant and flavorful when bruised or crushed. The flowers are considered to be inconspicuous.

The leaves can be harvested fresh or dried for teas, both hot and cold. They're also useful in flavoring desserts and savory dishes.

M. officinalis (above & below)

Features: fragrant; useful foliage **Height:** 24"
Spread: 18–24" **Hardiness:** zones 3–7

Mint

Mentha

M. x *piperata* 'Chocolate' (above)
decorative variegated variety (below)

The cool, refreshing flavor of mint lends itself to tea and other hot or cold beverages. Mint sauce made from freshly chopped mint leaves is often served with lamb.

A few sprigs of fresh mint added to a pitcher of iced tea give it an added zip.

Growing

Mints grow well in **full sun** or **partial shade**. The soil should be **average to fertile, humus rich** and **moist**. These plants spread vigorously by rhizomes and may need a barrier in the soil to restrict their spread.

Tips

Mints are good groundcovers for damp spots. They grow well along ditches that may only be periodically wet. They also can be used in beds and borders, but place mints carefully, because they may overwhelm less vigorous plants. Growing mints in decorative containers is an ideal way to keep them in check and stop them from spreading everywhere.

The flowers attract bees, butterflies and other pollinators to the garden.

Recommended

Many species, hybrids and cultivars of mint exist. Spearmint (*M. spicata*), peppermint (*M. x piperita*) and orange mint (*M. x piperita citrata*) are three of the most commonly grown culinary varieties. Other varieties have decorative variegated, curly or fruit-scented leaves.

Features: fragrant foliage; purple, pink or white summer flowers **Height:** 6–36"
Spread: 36" or more **Hardiness:** zones 4–8

Oregano • Marjoram

Origanum

Oregano and marjoram are two of the best known and most frequently used herbs. They are popular in stuffings, soups and stews, and no pizza is complete until it has been sprinkled with fresh or dried oregano leaves.

Growing

Oregano and marjoram grow best in **full sun**. The soil should be of **poor to average fertility, neutral to alkaline** and **well drained**. The flowers attract pollinators to the garden.

Tips

These bushy perennials make a lovely addition to any border and can be trimmed to form low hedges.

Recommended

O. majorana (marjoram) is upright and shrubby with light green, hairy leaves. It bears white or pink flowers in summer and can be grown as an annual where it is not hardy.

O. vulgare **var**. *hirtum* (oregano, Greek oregano) is the most flavorful culinary variety of oregano. The low, bushy plant has hairy, gray-green leaves and bears white flowers. Many other interesting varieties of *O. vulgare* are available, including ones with golden, variegated or curly leaves.

O. vulgare 'Aureum' (above & below)

In Greek, oros *means 'mountain' and* ganos *means 'joy,' so oregano translates as 'joy of the mountain.'*

Features: fragrant foliage; white or pink summer flowers; bushy habit **Height:** 12–32"
Spread: 8–18" **Hardiness:** zones 5–9

Parsley
Petroselinium

P. crispum (above), *P. crispum* var. *crispum* (below)

Although parsley is usually used as a garnish, it is rich in vitamins and minerals and is reputed to freshen the breath after garlic- or onion-rich foods are eaten.

Growing

Parsley grows well in **full sun** or **partial shade**. The soil should be of **average to rich fertility, humus rich, moist** and **well drained**. Direct sow the seeds, because parsley resents transplanting. If you start seeds early, use peat pots so the plants can be potted or planted out without disruption.

Tips

Start parsley where you intend to grow it, because it doesn't transplant well. Keep a container of parsley close to the house for easy picking. The bright green leaves and compact growth habit make parsley a good edging plant for beds and borders.

Recommended

P. crispum forms a clump of divided, bright green leaves. Because the leaves are the desired parts, not the flowers or the seeds, this biennial is usually grown as an annual. Both flat- and curly-leaved cultivars are available. Flat leaves like those of Italian parsley are more flavorful, and curly ones are more decorative. Dwarf cultivars are also available.

Features: attractive foliage **Height:** 8–24"
Spread: 12–24" **Hardiness:** zones 5–8;
treat as an annual

Rosemary
Rosmarinus

The needle-like leaves of rosemary are used to flavor a wide variety of culinary dishes, including chicken, pork, lamb, rice, tomato and egg dishes.

Growing

Rosemary prefers **full sun** but tolerates partial shade. The soil should be **well drained** and of **poor to average fertility**. Many rosemary selections are tender shrubs that should be moved indoors for winter, but several cultivars are true perennials in Tennessee.

Tips

Hardy rosemary selections are often grown in a shrub border. Low-growing, spreading plants can be included in a rock garden or along the top of a retaining wall or can be grown in hanging baskets. Plants grown in containers rarely reach their full mature size.

Recommended

R. officinalis is a dense, bushy, evergreen shrub with narrow, dark green leaves. Among the cultivars, the habit varies somewhat from strongly upright to prostrate and spreading. The flowers are usually in shades of blue, but pink-flowered cultivars are available. Cultivars that are winter hardy in Tennessee include **'Arp,' 'Athens Blue Spires,' 'Falling Waters,' 'Hill Hardy'** and **'Salem.'**

R. officinalis (above & below)

To overwinter a container-grown rosemary, keep it in very light or partial shade outdoors in summer. Then put it in a sunny window indoors for winter; keep it well watered but allow it to dry out slightly between waterings.

Features: fragrant, evergreen foliage; bright blue or pink summer flowers **Height:** 8"–4' **Spread:** 1–4' **Hardiness:** zones 8–10

Sage
Salvia

'Icterina' (above), 'Purpurea' (below)

Sage is perhaps best known as a flavoring for stuffings, but it has a great range of uses, and it is often included in soups, stews, sausages and dumplings.

Growing

Sage prefers **full sun** but tolerates light shade. The soil should be of **average fertility** and **well drained**. This plant benefits from a light mulch of compost each year and tolerates drought once established.

Tips

This attractive plant adds volume to the middle of a border or works as an attractive edging or feature plant near the front. Sage can also be grown in mixed planters.

Recommended

S. officinalis is a woody, mounding plant with soft, gray-green leaves. Spikes of light purple flowers appear in early and mid-summer. Many cultivars with attractive foliage are available, including the silver-leaved **'Berggarten,'** the yellow-margined **'Icterina'** and the purple-leaved **'Purpurea.'** The variegated **'Tricolor,'** which is purple, green and cream, has a pink flush to new growth.

Sage has been used since at least ancient Greek times as a medicinal and culinary herb and continues to be widely used for both those purposes today.

Features: fragrant, decorative foliage; blue or purple summer flowers **Height:** 12–24" **Spread:** 18–36" **Hardiness:** zones 5–8

Sweet Basil

Ocimum

The sweet, fragrant leaves of fresh sweet basil add a delicious, licorice-like flavor to salads and tomato-based dishes.

Growing

Sweet basil grows best in a **warm, sheltered** location in **full sun**. The soil should be **fertile, moist** and **well drained**. Pinch the tips regularly to encourage bushy growth. Plant out or direct sow seed after frost danger has passed in spring.

Tips

Although sweet basil grows best in a warm spot outdoors, it can be grown successfully indoors in a pot by a bright window to provide you with fresh leaves all year.

Recommended

O. basilicum is one of the most popular of the culinary herbs. Dozens of varieties are available, including ones with leaves that are large or tiny, green or purple and smooth or ruffled. Outstanding selections with showy and decorative flowers include 'African Blue,' 'Cinnamon' and 'Thai.'

O. basilicum cultivars (above & below)

Basil is a good companion plant for tomatoes—both like warm, moist growing conditions, and when you pick tomatoes for a salad, you'll also remember to include a few sprigs of basil.

Features: fragrant, decorative leaves
Height: 12–24" **Spread:** 12–18"
Hardiness: tender annual

Thyme
Thymus

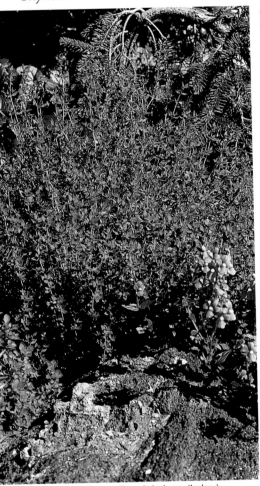

T. *vulgaris* (above), T. x *citriodorus* (below)

Thymes are popular culinary herbs used when cooking soups, stews, casseroles and roasts.

Growing

Thymes prefer **full sun**. The soil should be **neutral to alkaline** and of **poor to average fertility**. **Good drainage** is essential. It is beneficial to work leaf mold and sharp limestone gravel into the soil to improve structure and drainage.

Tips

Thymes are useful for sunny, dry locations at the fronts of borders, between or beside paving stones, in rock gardens, on rock walls and in containers.

Once the plants have finished flowering, shear them back by about half to encourage new growth and to prevent the plants from becoming too woody.

Recommended

T. x *citriodorus* (lemon-scented thyme) forms a mound of lemon-scented, dark green foliage. The flowers are pale pink. Cultivars with silver- or gold-margined leaves are available.

T. vulgaris (common thyme) forms a bushy mound of dark green leaves. The flowers may be purple, pink or white. Cultivars with variegated leaves are available.

Thyme plants are bee magnets when blooming. Pleasantly herbal, thyme honey goes very well with biscuits.

Features: bushy habit; fragrant, decorative foliage; purple, pink or white flowers
Height: 8–16" **Spread:** 8–16"
Hardiness: zones 4–9

Autumn Fern
Dryopteris

D. erythrosora

This lovely, easy-to-grow fern offers color, interest and a touch of class to any shady location.

Growing

Autumn fern grows best in **partial shade** but tolerates full sun in wet soil. The soil should be **fertile, humus rich** and **moist.** Divide the plant to control spread or to propagate.

Tips

The impressive autumn fern is useful in shaded areas and woodland gardens. It is ideal for sites that stay moist or periodically flood.

Recommended

D. erythrosora produces arching fronds 18–24" long. This fern is distinguished by its glossy foliage, bronze when young and maturing to a deep, dark green. It is very upright in form, and the foliage is supported by dark stems. The plant spreads by short, creeping rhizomes.

Autumn fern is one of the easiest ferns to grow and one of the hardiest.

Features: decorative fronds; upright growth habit **Height:** 24" **Spread:** 12–24" **Hardiness:** zones 5–9

Bugleweed
Ajuga

A. *reptans* 'Pat's Selection' (above)
A. *reptans* 'Caitlin's Giant' (below)

Often described as rampant runners, bugleweeds grow best where they can roam freely without competition.

Growing
Bugleweeds develop the best leaf color in **partial or light shade** and tolerate full shade, but too much sun can scorch the leaves. Any **well-drained** soil is suitable. Divide these vigorous plants any time during the growing season.

When growing hybrids with fancy leaf coloration, remove any new growth or seedlings that revert to green.

Tips
Bugleweeds make excellent groundcovers for difficult sites, such as exposed slopes and dense shade. They also look attractive in shrub borders, where their dense growth prevents the spread of all but the most tenacious weeds.

Recommended
A. **genevensis** (Geneva bugleweed) is an upright, noninvasive species that bears blue, white or pink spring flowers.

A. **pyramidalis** '**Metallica Crispa**' (upright bugleweed) is a very slow-growing plant with metallic, bronzy brown, crinkly foliage and violet blue flowers.

A. **reptans** (common bugleweed) is a low, quick-spreading groundcover. Its many cultivars are often chosen over the species for their colorful, often variegated foliage.

Combining well with hostas and ferns, bugleweed enjoys the same shady sites and growing conditions.

Features: colorful foliage; late-spring to early-summer flowers in shades of purple, blue, pink or white **Height:** 3–12" **Spread:** 6–36" **Hardiness:** zones 3–8

Christmas Fern

Polystichum

This evergreen fern is a treat, providing greenery year-round, not just during the Christmas season.

Growing

Christmas fern grows well in **partial, light or full shade**. The soil should be **fertile, humus rich** and **moist**. Remove dead and withered fronds in spring, before the new ones fill in.

Tips

Christmas fern makes an attractive addition to shaded beds and borders and can be included in a woodland garden. It is well suited to moist, shaded areas near a pond.

Recommended

P. acrostichoides forms a circular cluster of evergreen fronds that displays an arching habit. This species spreads with underground rhizomes and often has multiple crowns. Many cultivars are available, offering ruffled, crested or deeply toothed fronds.

P. acrostichoides (above & below)

A native of eastern North America, the hardy, low-growing Christmas fern is less invasive than many of its fern cousins.

Features: lush, ornate, evergreen foliage
Height: 12–24" **Spread:** 12–36"
Hardiness: zones 3–9

Cinnamon Fern
Osmunda

O. cinnamomea (above & below)

Ferns have a certain prehistoric mystique and can add a graceful elegance and textural accent to the garden.

Growing

These ferns prefer **light shade** but tolerate full sun in consistently moist soil. The ideal soil is **fertile, humus rich, acidic** and **moist,** but wet soil is tolerated. These plants spread by offsets that form at their bases.

Tips

When planted in large colonies, these large ferns form an attractive mass. They can be included in beds and borders, and they make a welcome addition to a woodland garden.

The flowering fern's 'flowers' are actually its spore-producing sporangia.

Recommended

*O. **cinnamomea*** (cinnamon fern) has light green sterile fronds that fan out in a circular fashion from a central point. Leafless, bright green fertile fronds that stand straight up in the center of the plant are produced in spring; they mature to cinnamon brown. This species produces skyward-reaching fronds 30"–5' long.

*O. **regalis*** (royal fern) forms a dense clump of foliage with size and form like those of *O. cinnamomea*. Feathery and flower-like, the fertile fronds stand out among the sterile fronds in summer and mature to a rusty brown. **'Purpurescens'** has purple-red sterile fronds that mature to green, contrasting nicely with the purple stems.

Features: deciduous, perennial fern; decorative fertile fronds; habit **Height:** 24"–5' **Spread:** 2–5' **Hardiness:** zones 2–8

Creeping Thyme

Thymus

T. serphyllum

Thyme tells everyone entering your garden that you're at the forefront of fashionable gardening trends, for this lovely petite perennial has left the herb jar and moved front and center as a highly valuable ornamental plant.

Growing

Creeping thyme prefers **full sun**. The soil should be **average to poor** and **very well drained,** but it helps to work leaf mold into it. Divide the plants in spring when necessary.

Tips

Creeping thyme is useful for sunny, dry locations at the fronts of borders as a groundcover, between or beside paving stones, in rock gardens and on rock walls. Plant it between stepping stones on pathways to create a fragrant, low-growing surface to walk upon without fear of killing the plants.

Recommended

T. serphyllum (creeping thyme, mother of thyme, wild thyme) is a popular low-growing species. It usually grows about 5" tall and spreads 12" or more. The flowers are purple. Many cultivars are available. **'Snowdrift'** has white flowers.

The large Thymus *genus has species throughout the world that have been used in various ways in a number of cultures. Ancient Egyptians used thyme for embalming, the Greeks added it to baths and the Romans purified their rooms with it.*

Features: fragrant, low-growing foliage; purple or white flowers **Height:** 5"
Spread: 12" or more **Hardiness:** zones 3–9

Dead Nettle
Lamium

L. maculatum 'Lime Light' (above), *L. maculatum* 'Beacon Silver' (below)

With its striking variegated leaves, dead nettle brightens up dark spaces. It looks especially lovely at dusk or in moonlight.

Growing

Dead nettle prefers **partial to light shade**; in full shade it may become leggy. The soil should be of **average fertility, humus rich, moist** and **well drained**. The more fertile the soil, the more vigorously the plant grows. Plant in spring or fall.

Dead nettle tolerates drought when grown in shade, but it can develop bare patches if the soil is allowed to dry out for extended periods. Divide and replant dead nettle in fall if bare spots become unsightly.

Tips

This plant is a useful groundcover in woodland or shade gardens. Or try planting it under shrubs in a border, where it will help keep weeds down.

Recommended

L. maculatum (dead nettle, spotted dead nettle) is a low-growing, spreading plant with white, pink or mauve flowers. Many cultivars are available.

Dead nettle remains more compact if sheared back after flowering. If the plant becomes invasive, pull some of it up, being sure to remove the fleshy roots.

Features: decorative foliage; white, pink or mauve flowers **Height:** 8" **Spread:** 36"
Hardiness: zones 3–8

Dwarf Plumbago
Ceratostigma

C. plumbaginoides (above & below)

When you add this late-blooming blue flower to the garden, remember where you plant it. Because it is one of the last plants to shoot up new foliage in spring, you have to be careful not to plop another plant right on top of it.

Growing

Dwarf plumbago grows best in **full sun** but survives with afternoon shade. It prefers **moist, well-drained** soil that is high in organic matter. Moderately drought tolerant once established, this quick-growing plant makes an excellent and tough ground-cover. Divide in spring.

Tips

Dwarf plumbago makes a wonderful addition to a rock garden, and it creeps happily between the rocks of a stone wall.

Recommended

C. plumbaginoides is a woody plant with erect stems. The foliage, which starts out light green highlighted with purple, becomes darker green as the outdoor temperature rises and then turns bronzy red in fall.

Features: blue flowers; attractive habit; fall color **Height:** 7–12" **Spread:** 15" **Hardiness:** zones 5–8

English Ivy • Ivy
Hedera

H. helix (above & below)

The soil should be of **average to rich fertility, moist** and **well drained**. The richer the soil, the better this vine grows. In a sunny, exposed site, the foliage can become damaged or dried out in winter.

Tips
Grown as a trailing ground-cover, English ivy roots at the stem nodes. As a climbing vine, it clings tenaciously to house walls, tree trunks, stumps and many other rough-textured surfaces, and the rootlets can damage walls and fences. English ivy can be invasive in warm climates. For slower growth, choose small-leaved cultivars.

Recommended
H. helix is a vigorous plant with triangular, glossy, dark, ever-green leaves that may be tinged with bronze or purple in win-ter, thereby adding another sea-son of interest to your garden.

Many cultivars have been devel-oped, some with interesting, often var-iegated foliage. Check with your local garden center to see what is available.

One of the loveliest things about English ivy is the variation in green and blue tones it adds to the garden.

Growing
English ivy prefers **light or partial shade** but adapts to any light con-ditions from full sun to full shade.

English ivy is popular as a houseplant, and it is frequently used in wire-frame topiaries.

Features: attractive foliage; climbing or trail-ing habit **Height:** 6–8" as a groundcover; up to 90' when climbing **Spread:** indefinite **Hardiness:** zones 5–9

Fairy Wings
Epimedium

*L*ong-lived and low maintenance with attractive heart-shaped, often colorful foliage and delicate sprays of orchid-like flowers, this plant is a woodland garden favorite.

Growing

Fairy wings grows best in **light or partial shade** but tolerates full shade. The soil should be **average to fertile, humus rich** and **moist,** but this plant is fairly drought tolerant once established. Cut back the foliage, especially if it looks tattered, before new growth begins in spring.

Tips

These spring-blooming plants are a popular addition to shade and woodland gardens, as accent plants or groundcovers. They can be planted under taller, shade-providing plants in beds and borders as well as in moist pondside situations. Fairy wings can be slow to establish, but they are worth the wait.

Recommended

Many species, hybrids and cultivars are grown for their attractive foliage and spring flowers. In habit, they vary from clump forming to spreading. *E.* x *cantabrigiense* is a clump-forming plant with dark green leaves and coppery orange flowers touched with

E. x *rubrum* (above & below)

red. *E. grandiflorum* is a clumpforming plant. Its cultivars have creamy white to dark pink flowers. *E.* x *perralchium* 'Frohnleiten' is a compact, spreading plant with bright yellow flowers and reddish green foliage that persists past fall. *E.* x *rubrum*, a low-spreading plant with small, wine- and cream-colored flowers, is one of the most popular groundcover selections.

With its single flowers, fairy wings adds an elegant accent to the garden; large groups make a dramatic display.

Also called: barrenwort, bishop's hat
Features: spring flowers in yellow, orange, cream, white, pink, red, purple or bicolored; often-colorful foliage; attractive habit
Height: 6–18" **Spread:** 12–24"
Hardiness: zones 4–8

Feather Reed Grass

Calamagrostis

'Overdam' (above), 'Karl Foerster' (below)

This graceful metamorphic grass changes its habit and flower color throughout the seasons. The slightest breeze keeps it in perpetual motion.

Growing

Feather reed grass grows best in **full sun**. The soil should be **fertile, moist** and **well drained**. Heavy clay and dry soils are tolerated. Rust is possible during cool, wet summers or with poor air circulation. Cut the plant back to 2–4" in very early spring, before growth begins. Divide reed grass if it begins to die out in the center.

Tips

Whether used as a single, stately focal point in small groupings or planted in large drifts, feather reed grass is a desirable, low-maintenance grass. It combines well with late-summer and fall-blooming perennials.

Rain or heavy snow may cause reed grass to flop temporarily, but it quickly bounces back.

Recommended

C. x *acutiflora* 'Karl Foerster' (Foerster's feather reed grass), the most popular selection, forms a loose mound of green foliage. The airy, distinctly vertical bottlebrush flowers emerge in June. Displaying a loose, arching habit when they first emerge, the flowering stems grow more stiff and upright over summer. Other cultivars include 'Overdam,' a compact, less hardy selection with white leaf edges. Watch for a recent introduction called 'Avalanche,' which has a white center stripe.

Features: open habit; fall color; winter interest; silvery, pink-and-tan flowerheads
Height: 3–5' **Spread:** 24–36"
Hardiness: zones 4–9

Fountain Grass

Pennisetum

The low maintenance needs and graceful forms of fountain grasses make them easy to place. They soften any landscape, even in winter.

Growing

Fountain grasses thrive in **full sun**. The soil should be of **average fertility** and **well drained**. Established plants tolerate drought. Plants may self-seed but are not troublesome. Shear perennials selections back in early spring and divide them when they start to die out in the center.

Tips

Fountain grasses can be used as individual specimen plants, in group plantings and drifts, or combined with flowering annuals, perennials, shrubs and other ornamental grasses. Annual selections are often planted in containers or beds for height and stature.

Recommended

Both perennial and annual selections are available. *P. alopecuroides* **'Hameln'** (dwarf perennial fountain grass) is a popular compact perennial cultivar with silvery white plumes and narrow, dark green foliage that turns gold in fall. (Zones 5–8) *P. glaucum* **'Purple Majesty'** (purple ornamental millet) is an annual with blackish purple foliage and coarse bottlebrush

P. setaceum 'Rubrum'

flowers. Its form resembles a corn stalk. *P. orientale* (Oriental fountain grass) is a perennial with tall, blue-green foliage and large, silvery white flowers (Zones 6–8, with winter protection) *P. setaceum* (annual fountain grass) is an annual with narrow, green foliage and pinkish purple flowers that mature to gray. **'Rubrum'** (red annual fountain grass) has broader, deep burgundy foliage and pinkish purple flowers.

Features: arching, fountain-like habit; silvery pink to purplish black foliage; silvery white, pinkish purple flowers; winter interest
Height: 2–5' **Spread:** 24–36"
Hardiness: zones 5–9

The name Pennisetum alopecuroides *refers to the plumy flower spikes that resemble a fox's tail. In Latin,* penna *means 'feather' and* seta *means 'bristle';* alopekos *is Greek for 'fox.'*

Golden Star
Chrysogonum

C. virginianum

This native perennial groundcover is found growing at the woodland's edge from southern Pennsylvania to Florida—a great indication of its preference for Southern climates and soils. It is sure to impress with its bright yellow blossoms that resemble mini sunflowers or zinnias.

Growing
Golden star does well in **full sun** if given **moist soil**. It tolerates well-drained soil in partial to full shade. Although the plant likes added humus, it isn't a requirement.

Tips
Because this perennial spreads by way of underground rhizomes, it is often used as a flowering groundcover. It could also be used at the front of perennial and shrub borders for a blast of bright color in early spring and continuing off and on through late fall.

Recommended
C. virginianum forms an attractive mat of toothed, coarsely textured foliage. Bright yellow, starry-shaped blossoms emerge in early spring and continue to appear sporadically until fall. A few cultivars are available with dark green leaves, wider spreads, longer blooming periods and more vigorous growth habits.

Chrysogonum *comes from the Greek* chrusos, *which means 'golden,' and* gonu, *which translates as 'knee.'*

Features: bright yellow flowers; lush foliage; attractive habit **Height:** 8–10"
Spread: 18–24" **Hardiness:** zones 5–8

Japanese Blood Grass

Imperata

Ornamental grasses have so much to offer in a Southern landscape, but adding color isn't often one of their strongest characteristics. This grass is here to say, 'Bring on the color!'

Growing

Japanese blood grass prefers **full sun** or **partial shade**. Any **moist** soil will do, as long as it's not wet.

Pull out any green-bladed plants that emerge from the clump. They will not turn red and have an aggressive to invasive nature.

Tips

Choose a location where the sun can filter through the leaf blades, so they appear to glow red. Sunny mixed borders are often best. This grass packs the most punch when planted in uneven groupings.

Recommended

I. cylindrica is a warm-season grass with upright, grassy growth. Its cultivars are well behaved, but the species is aggressive and invasive and is not commercially available. **'Red Baron'** (*I. cylindrica* var. *rubra*) produces somewhat translucent blades that emerge bright green with red tips. The red intensifies throughout the season, resulting in a deep wine red by fall. The foliage continues to change from one stunning color to another, turning to copper in winter.

I. cylindrica 'Red Baron' (foreground)

Japanese blood grass is also great to brighten up containers, adding a textural element offered by few other plants.

Features: colorful foliage; attractive size and form **Height:** 12–18" **Spread:** 12"
Hardiness: zones 6–9

Japanese Sweet Flag
Acorus

A gramineus 'Ogon' (above & below)

These grass-like plants are most at home in wet and boggy locations, making them a favorite of water gardeners.

Growing

Japanese sweet flags grow best in **full sun**. The soil should be **fertile** and **moist** or **wet**. Divide the plants for propagation and to prevent clumps from becoming too dense.

Tips

These plants are much admired for their habit as well as for the wonderful, spicy fragrance of the crushed leaves. Include Japanese sweet flags in moist borders or along pond margins. They can also be grown in containers.

Recommended

A. calamus (Japanese sweet flag) is a large, clump-forming plant that grows 2–5' tall, with about a 24" spread. The long, narrow, bright green foliage is fragrant. **'Variegatus'** is a popular and commonly available cultivar that has vertical yellow and cream stripes on its green leaves.

A. gramineus (Japanese rush, dwarf sweet flag) is a small, clump-forming plant. It grows 4–12" tall, with an equal spread, and bears fragrant, glossy, green leaves **'Ogon'** is prized for its bright, variegated, golden foliage. (Zones 5–8)

Japanese sweet flag was a popular moat-side plant in the past, and the fragrant leaves were spread on floors to keep rooms smelling sweet.

Features: attractive habit and foliage
Height: 4"–5' **Spread:** 4–24"
Hardiness: zones 4–8

Maiden Grass • Eulalia Grass

Miscanthus

One of the most widely grown ornamental grasses, maiden grass offers vivid colors and ornamental plumes while requiring little maintenance. Most of the vast array of selections available are hardy across Tennessee.

Growing

Maiden grass prefers to grow in **full sun** in **fertile, moderately moist, well-drained** soil, but it tolerates a variety of conditions.

Cut off dead, dried foliage to the top of the growing crown in mid-spring. Clumps can become quite large and may fall over from the weight of the foliage. It is best to divide them every 3–5 years to keep their size in check and maintain their appeal.

Tips

Maiden grass creates dramatic impact when massed in a naturalized area or mixed border. Some varieties can grow quite large and are best displayed as specimens. If left through fall and winter, the dried foliage and showy plumes look very attractive. Tall varieties make effective temporary summer screens.

Recommended

M. sinsesis is a perennial, clumping grass that spreads slowly from short, thick rhizomes. Its many cultivars and

M. sinsesis cultivars (above & below)

hybrids offer variegated, striped or speckled foliage of one or more colors, and ornate persistent, tall plumes. **'Gracillimus'** (maiden grass) has long, fine-textured leaves. **'Morning Light'** (variegated maiden grass) is a short, delicate plant with finely white-edged leaves. **'Strictus'** (porcupine grass) is a tall, stiff, upright selection with unusual yellow horizontal bands.

The fan-shaped plumes of maiden grass are ideal for cutting and for use in crafts and in fresh or dried arrangements.

Also called: Chinese silver grass, Japanese silver grass **Features:** colorful, strap-like foliage; showy plumes; winter interest
Height: 3–10' **Spread:** 2–5'
Hardiness: zones 3–8

Mondo Grass
Ophiopogon

O. *japonicus* (above)
O. *japonicus* 'Bluebird' (below)

Mondo grasses are excellent accent and contrast plants. The foliage provides the perfect dark background to highlight any brightly colored plant or flower.

Growing
Mondo grasses produce the best foliage in **full sun** but also grow in light shade. **Humus-rich, moderately fertile, moist, well-drained** soil is best. Divide in spring just as new growth resumes.

In zones 5 and 6, these plants appreciate thick mulch for winter protection.

Tips
Mondo grasses spread by rhizomes, making them good as dense groundcovers and for erosion control. Use them for border edges and containers. In cool zones they can be treated as bedding plants and, if desired, dug up and stored for winter in a cool, dark room.

Recommended
O. japonicus (mondo grass, monkey grass) produces grass-like, dark green foliage that grows 8–12" long and forms an evergreen mat of lush foliage that resembles an unkempt lawn. Short spikes of purple flowers emerge in summer, followed by metallic blue fruit. The many cultivars offer dwarf forms and variegated forms.

O. planiscapus 'Ebknizam' (EBONY NIGHT) (black mondo grass, black lily turf) has curving, almost black leaves and dark lavender flowers. It grows 4–6" tall and 6–12" wide. 'Nigrescens' has curving, almost black foliage and pink to white-flushed pink flowers. It grows 6–12" tall and 12" wide. Both cultivars produce blackish, berry-like fruit.

Mondo grasses belong to the same family as lilies and do not like being mowed.

Features: unusually dark foliage; groundcover habit; purple, lavender or pink flowers
Height: 4–12" **Spread:** 6–12"
Hardiness: zones 5–9

Monkey Grass • Lily Turf

Liriope

Often confused with mondo grass (*Ophiopogon* genus), these grass-like perennials are commonly used throughout the South because of their showy flowers, clump-forming growth habit and usefulness as groundcovers and for border edging.

Growing

Monkey grasses prefer **full sun** or **partial shade**. **Light, slightly acidic, moderately fertile, moist, well-drained** soil is best.

Tips

A row of monkey grass planted along a border edge creates a defined, ornate line separating the bed from a pathway, sidewalk, patio or driveway.

Recommended

L. muscari is a clump-forming perennial with arching, grass-like foliage. In late summer, flower spikes supporting bright purple flowers emerge from the crown. Cultivars are available with white flowers or variegated silvery or golden foliage. **'Big Blue'** bears violet blue flowers. **'Monroe White'** produces white flower spikes held above dark green foliage. **'Variegata'** produces green leaves with creamy yellow edges and purple flowers.

L. spicata is a creeping species that forms into a dense groundcover in

L. muscari (above)
L. muscari 'Variegata' (below)

almost no time at all. This species grows 8–9" tall. Cultivars are available with white or purple flowers and solid or variegated foliage.

The flowers of monkey grasses are followed by small, black, berry-like fruit.

Features: purple, violet blue or white flowers; grass-like foliage in dense clumps
Height: 8–24" **Spread:** 12–24"
Hardiness: zones 6–10

Ostrich Fern

Matteuccia

M. struthiopteris (above & below)

This fern is prized for its delicious emerging spring fronds as well as for its ornamental foliage and habit.

Growing

Ostrich fern prefers **partial** or **light shade** but tolerates full shade. The soil should be **neutral to acidic, average to fertile, humus rich** and **moist**.

Tips

This fern appreciates a moist woodland garden and is often found growing wild along the edges of woodland streams and creeks. Useful in shaded borders, it is quick to spread—to the delight of gardeners who have tasted the delicate young fronds.

Recommended

M. struthiopteris (*M. pennsylvanica*) forms a circular cluster of slightly arching sterile fronds. Stiff, brown fertile fronds poke up in the center of the cluster in late summer and persist through winter.

The tightly coiled new spring fronds of ostrich fern taste delicious lightly steamed and served with butter. Remove the bitter, papery, reddish brown coating before steaming.

Also called: fiddlehead fern
Features: perennial fern; attractive foliage and habit **Height:** 3–5' **Spread:** 12–36" or more **Hardiness:** zones 1–8

Pachysandra

Pachysandra

Low-maintenance pachysandra is one of the most popular groundcovers. Its rhizomatous rootzone colonizes quickly to form a dense blanket over the ground.

Growing

Pachysandra prefers **light to full shade** and tolerates partial shade. Any soil that is **acidic, humus rich, moist** and **well drained** is good. Plants can be propagated easily from cuttings or by division.

Tips

Pachysandras are durable groundcovers under trees, in shady borders and in woodland gardens. The foliage is considered evergreen but winter-scorched shoots may need to be removed in spring. Shear or mow old plantings in early spring to rejuvenate them.

P. terminalis (above & below)

Recommended

P. terminalis (Japanese spurge) forms a low mass of foliage rosettes. It grows about 8" tall and can spread almost indefinitely. **'Green Sheen'** has, as its name implies, exceptionally glossy leaves that are smaller than those of the species. **'Variegata'** has white margins or mottled, silvery foliage, but it is not as vigorous as the species.

Interplant this popular groundcover with spring bulbs, hostas or ferns, or use it as an underplanting for deciduous trees and shrubs with contrasting foliage colors.

Features: perennial, evergreen groundcover; attractive habit; fragrant, inconspicuous, white spring flowers **Height:** 8" **Spread:** 12–18" or more **Hardiness:** zones 3–8

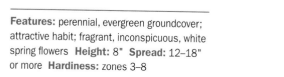

Pampas Grass
Cortaderia

C. selloana

This ornamental grass selection requires adequate space to reach its mature size without conflict, but its form and attractive plumes are worth making room for.

Growing

Pampas grass prefers **full sun** but tolerates light shade. **Fertile, well drained** soil is best, although any kind will do. Once planted, this grass requires little care. Established plants don't need fertilizer or supplemental watering. Division may be necessary however. Pampas grass should be thinned and cut back every spring, to a height of 24–36". If postponed for a number of years, the job may seem overwhelming.

Pampas grass is not reliably hardy in Tennessee and can be killed by extremely cold winters.

Tips

Pampas grass is usually integrated into the landscape for its dramatic flower plumes that last until they're cut down in spring. Pampas grass is ideal for dry slopes. Just make sure not to plant this stunner too close to walkways, patios or places with moderate to heavy foot traffic, because the blade edges are razor sharp and the plant can grow quite large.

Recommended

C. selloana is the true pampas grass; other species that are often sold as pampas grass are much weedier. This species produces sharply edged, grayish green leaves and tall, fluffy flower plumes in shades of tan. The species grows approximately 8–10' tall and 5–6' wide. Cultivars are available with variegated foliage or dwarf forms.

In order to distinguish the showier female specimens from the males, purchase pampas grass when the plumes are present.

Features: impressive size and form; flower plumes **Height:** 4–10' **Spread:** 4–10'
Hardiness: zones 8–10

Purple Muhly Grass

Muhlenbergia

The purple haze created by the flower plumes of purple muhly grass is sometimes mistaken for an unusual atmospheric phenomenon. It's bound to have you wanting more.

Growing

Muhly grasses thrive in **full sun** but tolerate light shade. **Well-aerated, well-drained** soil of just about any soil type is good. Established plants prefer infrequent watering.

For thicker clumps, leave the ripened seedheads in place to allow self-seeding. Otherwise, remove the seedheads before they ripen and fall. Muhly grasses can be cut back but are equally stunning when the new growth emerges through the previous year's growth.

Tips

These wild-looking, medium-sized grasses are perfectly suited to mixed beds and borders with bold-leaved plants that bring attention to their delicate appeal. They are also useful for naturalizing areas that receive little attention or care, and they work well as groundcovers for poor soil.

The fall colors are second to none and stand out when most other plants are looking spent.

Recommended

M. capillaris (Gulf muhlygrass, mist grass, hairy awn muhly, pink muhlygrass) produces a dense, knee-high

M. capillaris

stand of fine, wispy, grayish green grass. This showy clump can reach heights and spreads of 3–4'. Purplish flowerheads begin to emerge in late summer and last for up to two months. **'Regal Mist'** bears rosy pink flowers.

M. filipes (purple muhly grass) is very similar to *M. capillaris* in appearance but has stockier flowering stems and blooms later. This species is also more prolific, with the purple flowers often obscuring the leaves. It grows 24–36" tall, with an equal spread.

Features: attractive form; pink or purple seedheads in fall **Height:** 2–4' **Spread:** 24–36" **Hardiness:** zones 5–10

Because of its use in traditional fine basket weaving and sweet scent, M. capillaris *is known as sweetgrass in parts of the South.*

Ravenna Grass
Saccharum

S. ravennae

Ravenna grass is an excellent and problem-free four-season plant. It offers attractive spring, summer and fall foliage, fabulous plumes of flowers, and a sturdy enough structure to provide an interesting form all winter.

Growing
Grow ravenna grass in **full sun** in **moderately fertile, well-drained** soil. Provide **shelter** from strong winds. Established plants tolerate drought. Excessive fertility and overwatering can cause the stems to flop over.

Cut back the foliage and flowers in early spring to make room for new growth. Divide in spring or early summer to propagate more plants. Deadhead the flowers to prevent prolific self-seeding.

Tips
Ravenna grass is very effective as a specimen or accent plant. It can be used at the back of beds and borders as a textured backdrop for smaller, broadleaf plants or as a seasonal screen or hedge. The large flower spikes are used in fresh and dried arrangements.

Recommended
S. ravennae is a large, erect, clump-forming perennial grass with long, arching, strap-like, gray-green, white-striped foliage that turns orange to bronze in fall. The plume-like flowers are borne on tall, stiff stems that rise well above the foliage in late summer and early fall.

A large percentage of the world's sugar supply is derived from S. officinarum *(sugar cane), a close relative of ravenna grass.*

Also called: plume grass, hardy pampas grass **Features:** attractive foliage and growth habit; plume-like flowers; winter interest **Height:** 10–12' **Spread:** 3–6' **Hardiness:** zones 6–10

Sedge
Carex

'Sedges have edges' is the opening line to a classic gardener's poem that points out that this plant, unlike true grasses, has triangular stems. Sedge foliage comes in green, blue, rust, bronze or gold, allowing the gardener to add broad, colorful strokes or bright accents to the landscape.

Growing

Most sedges grow well in **full sun** or **partial shade** in **neutral to slightly alkaline, moist, well-drained** soil. '**Frosted Curls**' prefers average to dry soil and tolerates drought once established. Propagate by seed or division of clumps in mid-spring to early summer.

Tips

Use the colorful foliage and rustic texture of these grass-like plants in rock gardens, water features, containers and borders. The fine foliage of '**Frosted Curls**' contrasts well with coarse-textured plants.

Stems can be cut to the ground in early spring before new growth occurs, or they can be 'combed' to remove the older foliage.

Before collecting the seeds of sedges, allow the seedheads to dry on the plants.

C. comans 'Frosted Curls' (above)

Recommended

Many sedges are available. Check your local garden center's selection.

C. comans '**Frosted Curls**' (*C.* 'Frosted Curls'; New Zealand hair sedge) is a compact, clump-forming, evergreen perennial with fine-textured, very pale green, weeping foliage. The foliage appears almost iridescent, with unusual curled and twisted tips.

Features: interesting, colorful foliage; attractive habit **Height:** 10–18"
Spread: 12–15" **Hardiness:** zones 7–9

Strawberry Begonia
Saxifraga

S. stolonifera 'Kinki Purple' (above), *S. stolonifera* (below)

More than 400 species of *Saxifraga* are known, but *S. stolonifera* is probably one of the best selections for the South, for all it has to offer and its tolerance for excessive heat.

Growing

Strawberry begonia prefers **partial to full shade**. The soil should be **neutral to alkaline, fertile, moist** and **well drained**. Divide in spring.

This perennial groundcover is neither a begonia nor a geranium, but it displays physical characteristics reminiscent of both.

Tips

Strawberry begonia is an excellent addition to rock gardens and borders but also works well in shaded mixed borders. It can also be used as a groundcover in moist soil.

Recommended

S. stolonifera (strawberry geranium, mother of thousands) produces a thick, semi-evergreen mat of attractively gray-veined leaves with purple undersides, along with spikes of tiny white flowers. The parent plant sends out shoots, at the ends of which grow tiny new plants.

Features: white summer flowers; attractive foliage; spreading habit **Height:** 12–24"
Spread: 24" **Hardiness:** zones 7–9

Vinca
Vinca

Vinca is a dependable spreading groundcover, and a single plant can eventually cover almost any size area. Its reliability is second to none, and its ease of growth is sure to please.

Growing
Vinca grows best in **partial to full shade** in **fertile, moist, well-drained** soil. It adapts to many types of soil, but it turns yellow if the soil is too dry or the sun is too hot. Divide in early spring or fall, or whenever it becomes overgrown.

Tips
Vinca is a useful and attractive groundcover in a shrub border, under trees or on a shady bank, and it prevents soil erosion. This shallow-rooted plant can outcompete weeds but won't interfere with deeper-rooted shrubs.

If vinca begins to outgrow its space, it may be sheared back hard in early spring. The sheared-off ends may have rooted along the stems. These rooted cuttings may be potted and given away as gifts or introduced to new areas of the garden.

V. major (above), *V. major* 'Variegata' (below)

Recommended
V. major forms a mat of vigorous, upright to trailing stems bearing dark green, evergreen foliage. Purple to violet blue flowers are borne in a flush in spring and sporadically throughout summer. **'Variegata'** has foliage with creamy white edges.

Vinca is a great plant for use in mixed containers. As it drapes over the container edge, it dramatically enhances its companions' appearance.

Also called: greater periwinkle, myrtle
Features: trailing foliage; purple to violet blue flowers **Height:** 10–18" **Spread:** 18" to indefinite **Hardiness:** zones 6–9

Wintercreeper Euonymus
Euonymus

E. fortunei cultivars (above & below)

This evergreen creeper is well suited for use as a groundcover and acts as a living mulch around shrubs in mixed borders and beds.

Growing

Wintercreeper euonymus prefers **full sun** but tolerates light or partial shade. Soil of **average to rich fertility** is preferable, but any **moist, well-drained** soil will do.

If desired, wintercreeper euonymus can be grown as an evergreen shrub.

Tips

Wintercreeper euonymus can be grown as a climber with support or as a groundcover if left to trail along the ground.

Recommended

E. fortunei is rarely grown as a species; the wide and attractive variety of cultivars are preferred. They can be prostrate, climbing or mounding evergreens, often with attractive variegated foliage; BLONDY and 'Emerald Gaiety' are noted for their colorful foliage.

Features: attractive foliage
Habit: deciduous or evergreen groundcover or climber **Height:** 24"
Spread: indefinite **Hardiness:** zones 3–9

Glossary

Acid soil: soil with a pH lower than 7.0

Annual: a plant that germinates, flowers, sets seed and dies in one growing season

Alkaline soil: soil with a pH higher than 7.0

Basal leaves: leaves that form from the crown, at the base of the plant

Bract: a modified leaf at the base of a flower or flower cluster

Corm: a bulb-like, food-storing, underground stem, resembling a bulb without scales

Crown: the part of the plant at or just below soil level where the shoots join the roots

Cultivar: a cultivated plant variety with one or more distinct differences from the species, e.g., in flower color or disease resistance

Damping off: fungal disease causing seedlings to rot at soil level and topple over

Deadhead: to remove spent flowers to maintain a neat appearance and encourage a longer blooming season

Direct sow: to sow seeds directly in the garden

Dormancy: a period of plant inactivity, usually during winter or unfavorable conditions

Double flower: a flower with an unusually large number of petals

Genus: a category of biological classification between the species and family levels; the first word in a scientific name indicates the genus

Grafting: a type of propagation in which a stem or bud of one plant is joined onto the rootstock of another plant of a closely related species

Hardy: capable of surviving unfavorable conditions, such as cold weather or frost, without protection

Hip: the fruit of a rose, containing the seeds

Humus: decomposed or decomposing organic material in the soil

Hybrid: a plant resulting from natural or human-induced cross-breeding between varieties, species or genera

Inflorescence: a flower cluster

Male clone: a plant that may or may not produce pollen but that will not produce fruit, seed or seedpods

Neutral soil: soil with a pH of 7.0

Perennial: a plant that takes three or more years to complete its life cycle

pH: a measure of acidity or alkalinity; the soil pH influences availability of nutrients for plants

Rhizome: a root-like, food-storing stem that grows horizontally at or just below soil level, from which new shoots may emerge

Rootball: the root mass and surrounding soil of a plant

Seedhead: dried, inedible fruit that contains seeds; the fruiting stage of the inflorescence

Self-seeding: reproducing by means of seeds without human assistance, so that new plants constantly replace those that die

Semi-double flower: a flower with petals in two or three rings

Single flower: a flower with a single ring of typically four or five petals

Species: the fundamental unit of biological classification; the entity from which cultivars and varieties are derived

Standard: a shrub or small tree grown with an erect main stem, accomplished either through pruning and training or by grafting the plant onto a tall, straight stock

Sucker: a shoot that comes up from the root, often some distance from the plant; it can be separated to form a new plant once it develops its own roots

Tender: incapable of surviving the climatic conditions of a given region and requiring protection from frost or cold

Tuber: the thick section of a rhizome bearing nodes and buds

Variegation: foliage that has more than one color, often patched or striped or bearing leaf margins of a different color

Variety: a naturally occurring variant of a species

Index of Recommended Species Plant Names

Entries in **bold** type indicate main plant headings.

Abelia, 75
Abraham Darby,
   97
Acer, 83
Acorus, 158
Actinidia, 115
Ageratum, 11
Ajuga, 146
Akebia, 112
Allium, 134
Almond, dwarf
   flowering. *See*
   Prunus
American hop
   hornbeam, 59
Ampelopsis, 117
Andeli. *See* Double
   Delight
Anethum, 135
Angel wings. *See*
   Caladium
Antirrhinum, 29
Apricot, dwarf
   flowering. *See*
   Prunus
Aquilegia, 41
Aquilegia x *culto-*
   rum. See
   Columbine
Arborvitae, 60
   American, 60
   eastern, 60
   oriental, 60
   western, 60
Arrow-wood. *See*
   Viburnum
Artemisia, 35
Aster, 36
   Frikart's, 36
   New England, 36
   New York, 36
Autumn fern, 145
Azalea. *See* **Rhodo-**
   dendron

Bamboo, heavenly.
   See Nandina
Bamboo, sacred.
   See Nandina
Barberry, 61
   Darwin's, 61
   Japanese, 61
   Mentor, 61
Barrenwort. *See*
   Fairy wings
Beebalm, 37
Begonia, 12
   Rex, 12
   tuberous, 12
   wax, 12
Belamcanda, 119
Berberis, 61
Bergamot. *See* Bee-
   balm
Betty Boop, 101
Betula, 90
Bignonia, 111
Bishop's hat. *See*
   Fairy wings
Black gum, 62
Black lily turf. *See*
   Mondo grass
Blackberry lily, 119
Black-eyed Susan,
   38
Boxwood, 63
   common, 63
   edging, 63
   Korean, 63
Brassica, 17
Buddleia (Bud-
   dleja), 65
Bugleweed, 146
   common, 146
   Geneva, 146
   upright, 146
Burning bush, 64
Busy Lizzie. *See*
   Impatiens

Butter daisy, 13
Butterfly bush, 65
   alternate-leaved,
   65
   orange eye, 65
Buxus, 63

Caladium, 120
Caladium bicolor.
   See Caladium
Calamagrostis, 154
Calibrachoa, 32
Campsis, 108
Canna, 121
Capsicum, 23
Cardinal flower, 39
Carefree Beauty,
   97
Carex, 167
Carex 'Frosted
   Curls.' *See* Sedge
Carolina jes-
   samine, 107
Carolina silverbell,
   66
Catharanthus, 20
Catmint, 40
Cedar. *See*
   Arborvitae
   eastern redcedar,
   79
   eastern white
   cedar, 60
   western red
   cedar, 60
Celosia, 14
Cephalotaxus, 86
Ceratostigma, 151
Cercis, 88
Chamaecyparis, 70
Chamaemelum,
   133
Chamomile, 133

Cherry. *See* Prunus
   laurel, Carolina,
   87
   Higan, 87
   laurel, 87
   Potomac, 87
   Yoshino, 87
Chinese trum-
   petvine, 108
Chionanthus, 74
Chives, 134
   Chinese, 134
   garlic, 134
Christmas fern,
   147
Chrysogonum, 156
Cinnamon fern,
   148
   cinnamon, 148
   royal, 148
Clematis, 109
Clethra, 92
Climbing
   hydrangea, 110
Coleus, 15
Colocasia, 125
Columbine, 41
   alpine, 41
   Canada, 41
   common, 41
   European, 41
   hybrid, 41
   wild, 41
Common Blush
   China. *See* Old
   Blush
Coneflower, 42
   Tennessee, 42
Coneflower, cutleaf.
   See Black-eyed
   Susan
Coreopsis, 43
   bigflower, 43
   lance, 43